WHERE TODAY MEETS TOMORROW

Where Today Meets Tomorrow

EERO SAARINEN

and the

GENERAL MOTORS TECHNICAL CENTER

Susan Skarsgard

PRINCETON ARCHITECTURAL PRESS · NEW YORK

Published by
Princeton Architectural Press
202 Warren Street
Hudson, New York 12534
www.papress.com

Editor: Sara Stemen
Designer: Paul Wagner

Special thanks to: Paula Baver, Janet Behning, Abby Bussel, Jan Cigliano
Hartman, Susan Hershberg, Kristen Hewitt, Stephanie Holstein, Lia Hunt,
Valerie Kamen, Jennifer Lippert, Sara McKay, Parker Menzimer, Wes Seeley,
Rob Shaeffer, Jessica Tackett, Marisa Tesoro, and Joseph Weston of
Princeton Architectural Press
—Kevin C. Lippert, publisher

Library of Congress Cataloging-in-Publication Data
Names: Skarsgard, Susan, author. | Roche, Kevin, 1922– writer of foreword.
Title: Where today meets tomorrow : Eero Saarinen and the General Motors
    Technical Center / Susan Skarsgard.
Description: First edition. | New York : Princeton Architectural Press,
    2019. | Includes bibliographical references and index.
Identifiers: LCCN 2018050660 | ISBN 9781616897697 (hardcover :
    alk. paper)
Subjects: LCSH: GM Technical Center. | Saarinen, Eero, 1910-1961—
    Criticism and interpretation. | Modern movement (Architecture)—
    Michigan—Warren. | Business parks—Michigan—Warren. |
    Warren (Mich.)—Buildings, structures, etc.
Classification: LCC NA6233.W37 G467 2019 | DDC 720.9774/39—dc23
LC record available at https://lccn.loc.gov/2018050660

FRONT MATTER IMAGES:

2–3
Styling building and adjacent
fountain, 1963

4–5
Styling auditorium, viewed from
its patio, May 21, 2015

6–7
Exterior glazed-brick wall,
May 26, 2013

8–9
Central staircase, lobby of Research
administration building, May 11, 2013

10
Employees in the lobby of the
Styling administration building,
October 1, 1956

16–17
View of main entrance gate
from Mound Road, 1956

CONTENTS

FOREWORD

Kevin Roche

I was fortunate to join Eero Saarinen's office in early 1950. It was a very small office at the time—some ten or so architects. Eliel Saarinen, Eero's father, was still alive. He had received the commission for master planning the General Motors Technical Center (GMTC), and he contributed to the early direction the design took. Their combined efforts resulted in a completely original concept of assembling a group of workers with wide-ranging interests and housing them in separate buildings according to their specialties in such a way as to create a research village—a technical and design community.

In the years that followed, which were devoted to the detailed development of each building, an extraordinary number of innovations—such as the curtain wall design and the use of neoprene gaskets to make it watertight, as well as the five-foot module for walls, corridors, offices, and interior fittings—were to have a profound effect on the evolution of modern architecture worldwide. The assembly of these buildings around a central lake, a unifying element, was also a completely unique concept.

Eliel died early in the construction phase. Eero, with his boundless energy, took over the project and organized a staff to handle the largest construction project under-way anywhere at the time.

I was assigned to the Research building and given the task of studying the entrance lobby and its environs. Warren Platner was the architect in charge of the building and guided its evolution. I was able to propose the circular staircase in the lobby, and its development brought me into Eero's consciousness as the other projects in the office developed. I was privileged to participate with him in evolving original concepts. We had a wonderful relationship, and I feel that everything I learned about the practice of architecture I learned from Eero. (Although we didn't agree on everything: I was absolutely outraged at the idea of putting color on the brick walls. That was something Mies would never, ever have done, so I had to bend my head down and go with that one. Turned out, it was a great idea.)

Another participant in the design of the GMTC was John Dinkeloo, who was in charge of the technical developments for all of the buildings; he was responsible for many of the innovations in the construction. He and I worked closely together, and upon Eero's untimely death in 1961, we joined forces to complete all of his remaining projects and establish our own firm.

Smith, Hinchman & Grylls was the architect of record and was a very professional and accomplished group.

General Motors was a wonderful client. The people involved in the GMTC were all very positive and forward-looking. One person who stood out was Harley Earl, who in addition to offering his visionary guidance in car design was not shy about suggesting improvements in the architectural design.

Over time, General Motors had come to see the value of accommodating its employees in a way that would help them to be more productive and have a better life. That was as much an original idea as the architectural detailing of the new campus. Modern architecture is not about monuments, emperors, or popes—it's about people. And the GMTC demonstrates that very well because there's no nonfunctional building in the complex; there's no grand statement apart from the water tower. The Technical Center is very pragmatic.

It survives, and will continue to do so, as an extra-ordinary and sophisticated statement on the responsibility of architecture.

The history of the General Motors Technical Center is fundamentally a great American story. It's about important industrial leaders seeing the future and envisioning a place where ingenuity and intelligence would be nurtured and given free rein to support the consumer dreams of the postwar United States. It's about an architectural commitment to aesthetic purity and conceptual integrity. It's about true collaboration among client, architect, contractors, engineers, designers, suppliers, artists, and inventors.

I started working at GM Design in 1994, primarily on the design of emblems and nameplates for cars and trucks. In 2006 I received an assignment to design a commemoration of the fifty-year anniversary of the opening of the GMTC, a campus that was envisioned by the company's leadership as *the* place where new products, new techniques, and new industries would be studied and developed in an atmosphere that supported future product development. They wanted to build a place of significance both in its function and as an expression of their vision. My investigations into its amazing story launched a twelve-year study that ultimately led to the creation of this book. It also indirectly facilitated the formation of a new department: the GM Design Archive & Special Collections. It has been the profound privilege of my career to have been given the support to form and manage this organization that acquires, organizes, and makes accessible the history of automotive design at General Motors. In the larger context, I see this work as documenting *American* design history, given the influence that GM styling has had on our culture.

There are many beautiful books about important architectural projects. But this book stands out because it is written from the point of view of the client. The story is especially fascinating because the GMTC was Eero Saarinen's first large project and it established his method of working with clients to express *their* individual culture and identity. This approach translated into diverse architectural design solutions throughout his career,

which led to a great deal of criticism; for many years his eclectic strategy was seen as a sign of weakness or pandering to the client.[1] Over time, however, there has emerged a deeper understanding of Saarinen's work and his unique vision for purposeful architectural design.

The GM Technical Center was the project of a lifetime, and Saarinen embraced it by stepping out from his father Eliel's shadow to offer a reinterpretation of the International Style. He used the full resources of a generous and capable client to develop unique building methods and materials, many of which ultimately became standard practice in the industry. Together, client and architect developed a new modern aesthetic that was almost universally praised and generated immediate international acclaim.

Opening to great fanfare in 1956, the GMTC has functioned ever since as ground zero for the product development activities of General Motors. It is laid out much like a college campus, with the company's various disciplines housed in distinct buildings surrounding a man-made lake. Because of the proprietary nature of the work, it is a highly controlled environment that is usually closed to the public. This book is your invitation to see this great American landmark through historic and current photography that captures the essence of the campus and to read the surprising story of a thirty-eight-year-old untested architect who seized his moment to create one of the most important American architectural projects of the twentieth century.

CHAPTER ONE

GM History

As it planned its return to civilian business after World War II, General Motors was led by two very distinguished American industrialists: Alfred P. Sloan and Charles Kettering. They positioned GM to become the world's largest automotive company by adopting innovative manufacturing and production systems, an originative management structure, and technologically advanced research and development activities. They also understood and embraced design excellence as integral to the development of products that could satisfy postwar consumer demand. Sloan and Kettering felt it was essential to build a research and design facility where all product development activities would be in proximity to encourage the free range of thinking necessary for invention and innovation. They proposed the General Motors Technical Center, the largest and most architecturally significant campus of its kind at that time.

General Motors was founded by a flamboyant and daring entrepreneur, William "Billy" Crapo Durant (1861–1947), who helped lead the United States into the automobile age. A millionaire by the age of forty, Durant had made his fortune manufacturing horse-drawn vehicles. His Durant-Dort Carriage Company was the largest single producer of such vehicles at the turn of the twentieth century.[1] Although he is not often referred to in the same breath as Henry Ford, Walter P. Chrysler, or Alfred Sloan, the "king of Flint carriage makers" was an influential force in the early years of the American Motors Corporation, Chrysler Corporation, and General Motors.[2]

By all accounts, Durant was a colorful character—a consummate salesman and a charming visionary who used his carriage-industry fortune to begin acquiring automotive companies in 1904, when the financiers of the Buick Motor Company persuaded him to manage the struggling enterprise. He quickly recognized great economic potential in the fledgling automobile industry and used his carriage business know-how to steadily grow Buick, setting industry records and turning it into the largest automobile manufacturer in the United States.[3] By 1908 Durant's vision had grown beyond Buick. On September 16 of that year he incorporated the General Motors Company of New Jersey, and by the end of November General Motors had acquired both Buick and the Olds Motor Works. An automobile empire had begun. Durant continued his acquisitions spree and by 1910 had expanded to twenty-five firms.[4] But these acquisitions put the company deeply in debt; when it was on the brink of collapse, a group of bankers forced a deal on Durant to save General Motors from bankruptcy, and he lost control of his company.[5]

Durant's response to this colossal defeat was to form yet another company to compete head-on with Ford, which had a lock on the low end of the market with its Model T.[6] He joined forces with a renowned Buick

opposite
William Crapo Durant, ca. 1904

top left
General Motors Building,
127 Woodward Avenue,
Detroit, early 1900s

top right
William Durant (in vehicle, with cap)
in a 1906 Buick Model F, ca. 1906–7

bottom
Louis Chevrolet, 1911

race-car driver, Louis Chevrolet, to create the Chevrolet Motor Company. The honeymoon didn't last long, though; Durant and Chevrolet soon clashed over the direction of the company. The latter had dreams of building a large, powerful luxury vehicle, not an economy car. A final petty argument over Chevrolet's cigarette-smoking habits led to his departure from his namesake company.[7] Now solely in Durant's hands, Chevrolet focused on manufacturing lower-priced vehicles—a strategy that proved an almost immediate success.

Meanwhile, General Motors saw its share of the US market plunge from 20 percent in 1910 to less than 11 percent in 1915. In a bold move, Durant took advantage and managed to regain his stake in GM by trading his valuable Chevrolet stock. In 1916 he declared to the GM board of directors that he controlled the majority of the company's stock and was named president of General Motors.[8]

Over the next few years, the Durant-led GM acquired fourteen companies, including a controlling stake in Fisher Body, which provided the strategic advantage of bringing all body design and production in-house. Another of these acquisitions was a nonautomotive company called Guardian Frigerator Company of Fort Wayne, Indiana, which GM bought in 1919. It would become the market leader in home refrigerators under the brand name Frigidaire. The acquisition of Hyatt Roller Bearing Company, led by Alfred Sloan, would have a great impact on GM in the years to come. The implementation of Sloan's production system, based on anticipated demand, allowed for minimal inventory retention and a methodical production schedule.[9]

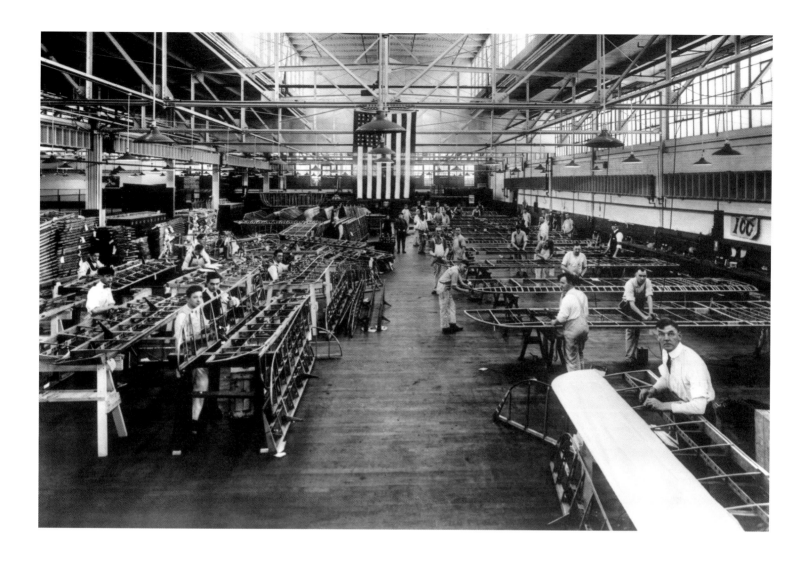

Another major innovation that General Motors introduced was vehicle financing. The General Motors Acceptance Corporation (GMAC), founded on January 29, 1919, introduced the concept of purchasing a car or truck on an installment plan. This released dealers from the burden of having to purchase the vehicles outright from the factory and made car ownership much more feasible for the average consumer.[10]

In April 1917 the United States joined the war that had ravaged much of the European continent for nearly three years. Although the relatively new automobile industry had no experience with military production, General Motors placed its facilities at the government's disposal, building trucks and ambulances, V-8 engines for artillery tractors, mortar shells, staff cars, and aircraft engines.[11]

Durant served as the president of GM from 1916 to 1920. At the time of his departure he was managing seventy-five factories in forty cities in the United States and Canada, with more than fifty executives reporting to him.[12] But losses outstripped gains, and GM experienced financial problems due to sluggish sales and the broader US economic recession that followed the temporary postwar boom. So severe were these problems that the construction of a new headquarters building in Detroit, designed by architect Albert Kahn, had to be halted. Ultimately, the company's major stockholders and financiers lost faith in Durant and forced him to cede control of GM for the last time, as the worsening recession and a falling stock price put GM on the verge of bankruptcy in 1920. (Durant stayed a dreamer nearly to the end, initiating other automotive

Aircraft production at Fisher Body plant in California, ca. 1917–18

ventures and a failed chain of family entertainment complexes; he died virtually penniless in 1947 at the age of eighty-five.)[13]

The early General Motors was a family of brands and operations whose unique strengths reinforced each other. It was also a maze of companies lacking coordination and accountability. After the 1920 financial crisis, GM refocused its operations to regain momentum and develop growth opportunities. The Durant era was over. Pierre S. du Pont, who was a major shareholder both personally and through his family's business, E. I. du Pont de Nemours and Company, had joined the GM board as chair in the aftermath of Durant's original departure. He then assumed the presidency and provided a stabilizing force. But it would be his second-in-command, Alfred Sloan, who really changed the future for GM.[14]

Alfred Pritchard Sloan Jr. (1875–1966) became GM's president on May 10, 1923. Sloan recognized that each of the business units needed a degree of freedom to be responsive and innovative, but also that accountability and central coordination would reduce redundancy and bloat. His vision for GM management was articulated in a study that emphasized the concept of decentralized operations and responsibilities with coordinated control.[15] GM's manufacturing divisions were given autonomy to innovate and build competitive products, while financial oversight and broad strategic direction came from central governing bodies. This system ultimately became a management model for large corporations worldwide and led to the idea of creating a campus that would centralize all product development activities.

In an era when all auto manufacturers followed a mass-production paradigm, GM proved more nimble than the competition in developing new products and implementing plant changes. For instance, GM established a policy to ensure that all the technical and styling advances made by the divisions each year would be rolled into the production process at one time, thus initiating the now-ubiquitous "annual model change."[16] This concept was not without controversy when it was first introduced; however, instituting a process that recognized and regulated necessary change was among the many factors that gave GM a competitive edge in the market during the twentieth century.

Sloan's greatest contribution to General Motors and the broader auto industry was his idea that offering distinctive brands and models at graduated price points would direct consumers' aspirations.[17] This market segmentation was promoted to the public as "a car for every purse and purpose."[18] Sloan was also the first to recognize that styling and technological features were becoming distinguishing elements in the buyer's mind. He enlisted innovators such as Charles Kettering and Harley Earl to keep General Motors' products ahead of the competition's. This understanding of the importance of design would later influence the selection of the architect for the company's Technical Center.

Charles Franklin "Boss" Kettering (1876–1958) was GM's first vice president of Research and served from its founding in 1920 until his retirement in 1947. Durant had originally lured him in 1916 with an offer too good to resist: to create and organize GM's Research Laboratories. Kettering sold his Dayton Engineering Laboratories Company (DELCO)—responsible for innovations such as the self-starter, which eliminated the dangers of crank-starting—to Durant's United Motors Corporation and became vice president of the General Motors Research Laboratories within weeks of Durant's final departure in 1920. In 1925 the laboratories moved to Detroit. Given the opportunity to freely pursue any and all ideas to improve the automobile, he set out on a legendary career of research and development innovation.

Kettering functioned as a sort of spark plug. He was a prolific inventor, engineer, and businessman and the holder of 185 US patents.[19] He was responsible for a staggering list of inventions, many of which GM brought to market in its products. These included the aforementioned 1912 electric self-starter; leaded, antiknock gasoline (in 1921), which allowed engines to run more efficiently and at higher octane; long-lasting, quick-drying Duco lacquers and enamel finishes (in 1924), which broadened the spectrum of colors available for automotive exteriors; Freon, the development of which began in 1926, for

opposite top
Construction of the General Motors Building, designed by Albert Kahn, Detroit, May 17, 1920

opposite bottom
Executive portrait of Alfred Sloan, undated

above left
Executive portrait of Charles Kettering, undated

above right
Charles Kettering with his self-starter on its twenty-fifth anniversary, 1937

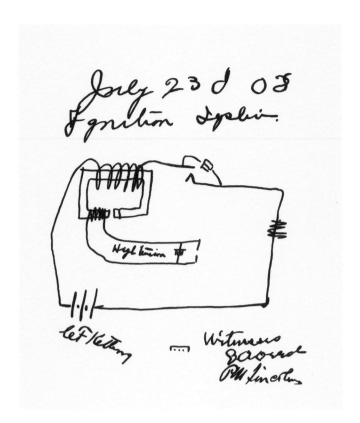

The CAR
THAT HAS NO CRANK

refrigeration and air conditioning; and high-compression engines (in 1948), which provided greater power for automobiles in the age of US interstate highway expansion.[20] These and many other inventions directly influenced the proliferation of the automobile in the United States by making it safer, more comfortable, and more convenient to operate. They also led to a continuous lowering of manufacturing costs and thus lower consumer prices.

Kettering's curiosity, creativity, and determination were legendary at GM, as were the processes he employed to achieve his many innovations. Sloan said of him, "He has been an inspiration to me and to the whole organization, particularly in directing our thoughts and our imagination and our activities toward doing a better job technically and the tremendous importance of technological progress."[21] Kettering was perhaps the single most important figure in the history of the corporation, and the fundamental idea of what the GM Technical Center could be originated in his correspondence with Sloan.

Harley Jefferson Earl (1893–1969) was a California-based industrial designer who made his reputation building custom-bodied Cadillacs for the Hollywood elite. His father, J. W. Earl, started a Los Angeles coach-building company called Earl Carriage Works in 1889 and rebranded it the Earl Automobile Works in 1908, the same year Durant formed the early General Motors.[22] Harley Earl worked for his father and gradually took over greater responsibility for the shop. The earliest vehicles designed and built by the Earls were highly modified standard models, differentiated through streamlining, custom accessories, or unique paint treatments.[23] Early film stars Fatty Arbuckle, Mary Pickford, and Douglas Fairbanks were among the company's high-profile customers.[24] It was at the 1919 Los Angeles Automobile Show that GM executives first noticed the Earls' work.[25] The Earl company's most important customer then was Los Angeles Cadillac dealer Don Lee. After years of using the Earl Automobile Works for custom bodywork, Lee acquired the company in 1919 and the expertise of Harley Earl along with it.

At the time, Lawrence P. Fisher was president of GM's Cadillac division under Alfred Sloan, and it was Fisher who first brought Harley Earl to Detroit.[26] In 1926 Earl was hired by contract with GM's Fisher Body division to design the exterior body for the 1927 LaSalle. In order to fill gaps in the price ladder, GM introduced what it called companion cars, which were in essence a sub-brand; this vehicle was to be Cadillac's entry for the lower end of the luxury-car market segment.[27] What Earl had been doing for the movie stars, Sloan wanted to do for GM. This was GM's first production automobile designed by a stylist, as opposed to an incremental change to an existing vehicle produced by engineers.[28] The styling of the 1927 LaSalle was influenced enormously by the European Hispano-Suiza, a personal favorite of Earl's.[29] It is notable that Earl presented GM leadership with four different body proposals for the LaSalle in the form of full-size clay models; he had used a similar technique when selling custom bodies in Hollywood, and it would soon become standard practice at General Motors.[30]

The 1927 LaSalle, available in a variety of body types and Duco paint colors, was revealed to the public at the Boston Auto Show in March 1927.[31] Design awards and impressive sales soon followed, and GM hired Earl as one of the industry's first full-time designers.[32] Sloan proposed the creation of the new Art and Colour section on June 23, 1927, and invited Earl to lead it.[33] In his memoir of his career at General Motors, Sloan wrote:

> I was so impressed with Mr. Earl's work that I decided to obtain the advantages of his talents for other General Motors car divisions....I took up with the Executive Committee a plan to establish a special department to study the question of art and color combinations in General Motors products....Mr. Earl's duties were to direct general production body design and to conduct research and development programs in special car design.[34]

Two women in the 1927 LaSalle Series 303 roadster, the very first LaSalle model, 1927

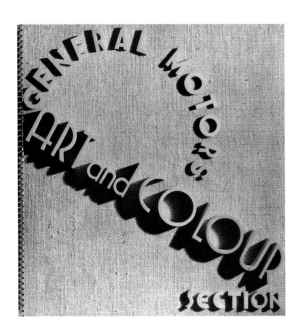

top left

The Development of the 1934 LaSalle:
A Short Story of the Activities of the
Art and Colour Section of General
Motors Corporation, ca. 1934

top right

Designers working on instrument
panels and body designs for the
1934 LaSalle in the Cadillac studio
in the Argonaut Building, Detroit,
early 1930s

bottom

Engineers working on a full-size
model of the 1942 Chevrolet Fleetline
sports sedan at the Argonaut Building
in Detroit, late 1930s

Earl initially struggled to legitimize the new department in an atmosphere in which "engineering was the all-absorbing activity and the engineer was usually the dominant personality."[35] Sloan provided no direction for the new department, instead trusting Earl to operate autonomously.[36] He had to find artists, engineers, and tradespeople with the skills to design stylish and functional vehicles at a time when no schools offered curricula supportive of this new discipline. In addition to identifying key existing GM employees for the new department, Earl hired trained architects, interior decorators, and advertisement illustrators; by 1928 he had assembled a staff of fifty designers and draftspeople.[37] William L. Mitchell, who eventually succeeded Earl, was hired from the art department at Collier's advertising agency.[38] Many of these artists and illustrators had very little knowledge or understanding of the technical requirements of automobile engineering or manufacturing.

Impact and credibility at GM took time for Earl, but his staff grew with each success, eventually organizing into studios for each of GM's existing passenger car brands—Cadillac, Buick, Oldsmobile, Pontiac, and Chevrolet—as well as studios for commercial trucks and other products.[39] His team set out to design new and distinctive brand identities for each of these divisions. By the end of the 1930s, Earl strove to make the automobile "longer, lower, and wider."[40] His concepts of clean lines and curves, fenders that flowed smoothly into side body panels, and one-piece steel roofs would transform the aesthetics of the automobile.

Original rendering of the 1937 LaSalle V-8 by William L. Mitchell

Turret-top roof panels for 1946
Chevrolets, January 23, 1945

Earl's Art and Colour section quickly outgrew its space at GM's headquarters in Detroit and moved to the Research Annex, later known as the Argonaut Building. Designed by Albert Kahn and constructed in two parts in 1928 (Research Annex A) and 1936 (Research Annex B), the building originally constructed for GM's Research laboratories would now house both its research and design operations. The eleven-story red-brown brick and limestone art deco high-rise stood adjacent to the General Motors Building, also designed by Kahn. In this new space the studios for each automotive division occupied a separate floor. Vehicle models were transported via elevator to the rooftop for evaluation in natural light.[41] (Both of these Kahn buildings still stand in Detroit. The General Motors Building was designated a National Historic Landmark in 1978, leased by the State of Michigan in 1998, and renamed Cadillac Place. The Argonaut Building was listed on the National Register of Historic Places in 2005. General Motors donated the building in 2007 to the College for Creative Studies, which renamed it the A. Alfred Taubman Center for Design Education in 2009.)

In 1937, around the same time it moved to its new residence in Research Annex B, the Art and Colour section was renamed Styling in recognition of its leading role in the newly developed disciplines of automotive and industrial design.[42] Besides designing the vehicles themselves, Earl directed the design of auto exhibits, experimental cars, streamlined trains, electric fans, batteries, radios, and all Frigidaire appliances manufactured by General Motors. He and his staff created the first "dream car" in 1938, called the Y-Job—a two-passenger convertible with a dramatically low-slung body. Its design forecasted the new styling and technologies to come: an absence of running boards, strong horizontal lines and complex curves, hidden headlamps, electric windows, a power-operated top, flush door handles, curved-glass door windows, and push-button door latches. It is widely considered the predecessor of all experimental cars that followed.[43]

left
Exterior view of the Argonaut Building, Detroit, designed by Albert Kahn, ca. 1930

right
Exterior view of the General Motors Building, Detroit, designed by Albert Kahn, ca. 1921–22

Earl had just as great an impact on the field of automotive design as he did on the products his team created; he is credited with establishing the very concept of the modern automotive design organization. He introduced countless methods of ideation and visual communication as standard design practice. These included the use of clay modeling, which provided a wider scope for innovative bodywork than the traditional plaster-and-wood method of sculpting. The clay models allowed for the visualization and modification of the 3-D form based on dimensional surface-development drawings. A wooden armature, complete with wheels, was built as a structure for support. Warmed modeling clay was then applied to the armature, and wooden templates were used to smooth and define the surface. Earl developed techniques that made the clay models look amazingly real: metallic foil applied to the clay surface to simulate chrome, blackout windows, and sheets of colored plastic that looked like lacquer paint.[44]

Earl's studios functioned as a training ground for talented designers who would go on to become leaders in the field of automotive design, including William L. "Bill" Mitchell, possibly his most important protégé, who succeeded him as vice president of Styling at General Motors from 1959 to 1977 and built on the design legacy that Earl had established.[45] Earl also fostered a close relationship between schools and the corporate design studios and even got involved in developing the curricula of Pratt Institute in New York, ArtCenter College of Design in Pasadena, Cleveland Institute of Art, and the Center for Creative Studies in Detroit.[46]

Buick Y-Job show car at the Argonaut
Building, Detroit, May 22, 1940

GM's board of directors elected Earl vice president of Styling on September 3, 1940, elevating his status in the company and solidifying his department's position as equal to that of Engineering and Research.[47] The years to come would include such trendsetting innovations as the pillarless hardtop, wraparound windshields, and tail fins. But these symbols of US growth and prosperity would not come until GM and the rest of the country returned to civilian life after World War II.

Perhaps the practiced ability of GM to embrace and harness change facilitated its efforts during the war:

> Once the United States officially entered the war, no company converted faster or more comprehensively to wartime production than General Motors. It has been called the greatest industrial transformation in history, with all of the General's 200-plus North American plants shifting to production of airplanes, tanks, machine guns....General Motors alone supplied the U.S. forces with military goods worth more than $12 billion....This was far more than any other company contributed.[48]

Sloan believed that "victory would come down to which nation performed best in the industrial realm" and marshaled every corporate resource to support the war effort.[49] General Motors' large number of strategically located production centers, the diversity of its operating facilities, and the technical quality of its personnel and engineering talent all contributed to its enormous potential for the production of war matériel. All civilian research, engineering, design, and production came to an abrupt halt. GM made a full conversion to military production and became a potent force in the creation of the nation's wartime arsenal. On February 1, 1942, the last passenger car rolled off the line.[50] The first postwar car would not roll off the line until forty-five days after V-J Day.[51]

left
An employee guides the lowering of a finished tank onto a train car in the Fisher Body plant in Grand Blanc, Michigan, May 7, 1945

right
Cadillac war bonds advertisement, 1942

GM marshaled its enormous resources under the direction of manufacturing genius William S. Knudsen, former president of the company, who was entirely in charge of war production on the home front after heeding the call of President Franklin D. Roosevelt.[52] In total, GM produced $12.3 billion worth of military airplanes, tanks, engines, trucks, and weapons for the "Arsenal of Democracy."[53] It also trained a total of 750,000 employees, far more than were needed to replace the workers who had enlisted in the service. Of these new employees, more than one-fourth were women and nearly all had little or no manufacturing experience when they arrived.[54]

As the end of the war neared, Sloan recognized that the next challenge would be leading the corporation's transition from a war to a peace economy— a changeover that would require reorganizing practically every aspect of the business. He began corresponding about the future of the company and its product development operation with his close friend and colleague Kettering. In a letter dated March 29, 1944, Sloan wrote:

> My dear Ket: I have been thinking about certain Corporation problems as affecting the long-term position of our affairs and I would like to ask your point of view, if I may, on one of these problems as I see it....I would visualize the physical development of this activity to consist of a set-up, close to, but outside, the City of Detroit. The Proving Ground would be desirable, but it is probably too far away for contact. It is, of course, immaterial where it would be located, as that is a matter of detail. I[t] would have a big enough place to carry on under one roof, all the essential component activities that I am talking about. I believe that such a set-up properly organized and administered, would serve to reduce the time element in bringing into our products, advanced research work of our own Research Department and otherwise.[55]

A letter dated April 11, 1944, to Kettering from E. V. Rippingille, a mechanical engineer and Kettering's right-hand man, read:

> I agree heartily with Mr. Sloan that the Product engineering group should be fortified with better facilities. I believe they are staffed in the most able manner and the effect of their technical advancement upon the Divisions will be more promptly realized thru acquired authority in matters of engineering policy as soon as they are given adequate support. Research will cooperate toward this end thru contributions in the field of engineering science.[56]

This is where the story of the General Motors Technical Center begins.

An employee inspects shell
cases at a Fisher Body war
conversion factory in Grand
Blanc, Michigan, 1945

CHAPTER TWO

Eliel Saarinen

In light of anticipated demand, General Motors' leadership prioritized its immediate return to large-scale manufacturing of its civilian products after the war. These included not only passenger cars and trucks but also automotive accessories, diesel engines for locomotive and marine vessels, and home appliances. To this end, the company contemplated a program to modernize and expand its facilities "to meet postwar needs and help assure its continued technical progress in automotive and related fields."[1] The General Motors Technical Center would be a key component of this plan.

Alfred Sloan recognized that in addition to requiring more modern production facilities, the company's central product development groups—Engineering, Research, and Styling—needed a space where they could carry out their work in proximity to one another to effectively translate important wartime technological advances to civilian applications. These staffs had outgrown their prewar facilities in Detroit and were scattered across the area in makeshift homes in various manufacturing buildings.[2] Sloan proposed his initial idea for what would become the General Motors Technical Center in March 1944. Over the course of the next month, he and Charles Kettering formulated a plan. On April 13 Sloan named the new facility:

> Let's set up what we would call—GENERAL MOTORS TECHNICAL CENTER....
> The center to which I have referred would comprise an expanded Research activity
> as defined by Mr. Kettering; and Engineering activity which would comprise
> Harley Earl's body design, correlated with the broadened product activity such as
> we are now conducting in Detroit.[3]

Many months before the end of the war, even before it had been formally announced to the rest of GM's leadership, Sloan's plan was in motion. Land acquisition was among the first considerations for the Technical Center campus, and approval was given to search for possible sites across the greater Detroit region. The desired location was to be "outside of highly congested areas, near a railroad, twenty-five to thirty minutes from the General Motors Building, and adjacent to residential areas."[4]

The township of Warren was approximately twelve miles from the General Motors Building in Detroit. With its central cluster of farms and flat topography, it met most of the criteria. In November 1944 authorization was given to option the land for purchase from Mound Road east to the railroad and from Twelve Mile up to Thirteen Mile, most of which was a farm called Clearview, owned by the Halmich family. The eighty-eight-acre plot was purchased in 1944 for $750 per acre. In 1950 and 1951 additional purchases led to a total of approximately 813 acres held by GM in Warren Township.[5]

opposite
Eliel Saarinen, June 1933

above
Plant conversion for Chevrolet truck and military vehicles, Norwood, Ohio, April 9, 1945

Schoolhouses viewed from
Mound Road facing southeast,
Warren, Michigan, April 16, 1946

On December 13, 1944, at a meeting of the GM Administration Committee in Detroit, Sloan went on record to those in attendance with his plans to establish "a technical center in line with the corporation's policy of improving its technological position" in the vicinity of Detroit:

> The plans are in a tentative stage and complete data will be submitted at a later date. It is proposed that the center shall house the present activities carried on by the Research division and the Art and Colour section; and also provide facilities for engineering research of a character comparable to the present product studies carried on by the central office engineering staff that are neither research activities presently carried on by the research division nor the individual engineering work carried on by the various divisional engineering groups.[6]

The proposal was enthusiastically received by the committee, which in addition to Sloan included two future board chairs, Albert Bradley and Frederic G. Donner, as well as Harlow H. Curtice, the future GM president who would eventually preside over the Technical Center dedication in 1956.[7]

Much initial discussion among GM's leadership centered on seeking and selecting the architect for the project. Some thought it best that GM itself should design the campus—that the architects of its in-house real estate division, Argonaut Realty Corporation, or an outside engineering firm would have the best expertise and knowledge to design the center exactly as the corporation would want.[8] Sloan and Kettering understood the importance of architecture for the image, spirit, and mission of a company and were impressed with the work of Albert Kahn, especially after Sloan visited the Kahn-designed Ethyl Corporation laboratories in Detroit. Albert Kahn Associates had been among the first to

use reinforced concrete to create large volumes of unobstructed space. In 1905 they had designed the first automobile factory in the world for Packard using this new technology. That led to Ford Motor Company's Highland Park plant in 1908 and in 1917 its famed River Rouge Complex in Dearborn, the largest US manufacturing facility at the time. By 1937 Kahn's firm was responsible for nearly 20 percent of all architect-designed factories in the United States.[9] They had also designed many lavish and important buildings throughout the Detroit area, including the Fisher Building, the Detroit Athletic Club, the General Motors Building, and the University of Michigan Central Campus. Kahn had been involved with noted industrial designer Norman Bel Geddes in designing GM's Futurama pavilion for the 1939 New York World's Fair, widely regarded as the most spectacular exposition ever held in the United States.[10]

GM Futurama exhibit at the New York World's Fair, 1939

Albert Kahn's Ethyl Corporation
building, Ferndale, Michigan, 1942

From the beginning, Harley Earl likewise argued in favor of hiring a skilled, forward-thinking architect of stature who could make the Technical Center a significant aesthetic statement; in the end, he was given the task of selecting the architect.[11] Earl recruited LeRoy Kiefer to assist in the selection process. Kiefer was an industrial designer working for Earl at the time, as well as a graduate of the University of Michigan's architecture program, and he had previously spent four years working for Kahn. (Kiefer would go on to serve in the instrumental role of head of the Product and Exhibition Design studio, which provided interior design work for the finished Technical Center buildings.) Earl and his team visited several leading schools of architecture to seek opinions and found that the Saarinens were universally recommended.[12] Kiefer was "deeply influential in the selection of the Saarinens"; however, Earl still needed to convince the leadership and board of directors.[13]

Earl saw the proposed Technical Center campus design as essential to the future of GM products and felt that the architecture should reflect the company's prioritization of style and advanced engineering. According to interior automotive designer George Moon, who worked at GM from 1954 to 1987, "Kettering was skeptical and actually against the idea of this center being taken in an aesthetic-driven direction. He feared the results would be a frivolous, non-functional group of buildings and divert from the seriousness and fundamental purpose of the center." Kettering wanted structures that would manifest the rigorous intellectual effort involved in the work, to telegraph that sense of gravity to both the employees inside and the public outside.[14] Kettering also had concerns about the competence of non-GM architects to design a laboratory building for their specific technical requirements. The dissonance between client and architect during the delicate negotiations were described in detail by C. F. Huddle, who worked directly for Kettering on the Technical Center project:

Bob Swanson was making the presentation of this preliminary plan. Eliel was there, Eero was there and I was there, and Rip [E. V. Rippingille] and the Boss [Kettering] were there and maybe some others, I don't remember. I knew something was going to happen. Finally, the Boss got up and said, "You fellows don't know anything about research requirements. How can you tell us how to plan a building? It just isn't in the books, it just isn't possible. You fellows don't know enough about it." I liked both of these fellows very well and I was really embarrassed. I couldn't take my eyes off the floor. Then Eliel got up and he said, "Mr. Kettering, I think you should get somebody else to do this job. We don't want it." I think that was the only time I was ever embarrassed for something I thought the Boss shouldn't have done.[15]

Lammot du Pont, longtime director and former GM board chair, also expressed his concerns in a letter to Sloan:

The whole layout and description of its preparation gave me the impression that the matter of esthetic treatment, or as I would style it, "dressing up the place," had been an important factor from the beginning. I questioned whether the matter of appearance was of any importance to a project of this kind, the sole object of [sic] being to get technical results.[16]

Du Pont went on to express his belief that an engineering firm—or GM engineers themselves—would be best suited to organizing the layout of the new facility. But Sloan was ultimately able to persuade him that a reputable architectural firm would be better. Du Pont relented: "I understand from your letter that it is not the intention to allow the appearance to interfere with the technical possibilities or to add substantially to the cost of the project. With those two assurances, my only remaining question with respect to the project would be answered."[17]

Moon speculated that Kahn had also submitted a proposal: "Albert Kahn, who had worked closely with Argonaut over the years, made their proposal

Architectural firm Saarinen and Swanson, May 1939. Left to right: Eero Saarinen, consultant; Eliel Saarinen, principal; and J. Robert F. Swanson, principal

Eliel Saarinen's drawing for his second-place entry in the 1922 Tribune Tower competition

through Argonaut, [although] admittedly, [Argonaut] was not staffed to handle a job the size and character of this project, particularly in the type of architect that would develop significantly forward-looking building concepts."[18]

Ultimately, Earl convinced Sloan and Kettering that the architectural firm Saarinen and Swanson of Bloomfield Hills was the right choice. The principals were the internationally renowned architect Eliel Saarinen and his son-in-law, J. Robert F. Swanson.[19] Eliel's views about the field of architecture were a prescient embodiment of much of what the project would involve:

> In my crystal ball, I see that during the next half of the century the time of collaboration between the clients, the financier, the lawyer, the politician and the architect-planner will be required to meet the manifold problems which lurk ahead....Architecture embraces the whole form-world of man's physical accommodations, from the intimacy of his room to the comprehensive labyrinth of the large metropolis. Within the broad field of creative activities, the architect's ambition must be to develop a form language expressing the best aims of his time—and of no other time—and to cement the various features of his expressive forms into a good interrelation, and ultimately into the rhythmic coherence of the multi-formed organism of the city.[20]

Eliel Saarinen (1873–1950) was born in Rantasalmi, Finland.[21] He was well known in Europe as an architect, city planner, and founder of the Finnish National Romantic school.[22] In 1922, then forty-nine years old, he had entered an international architectural competition to design a new office tower for the *Chicago Tribune*. The competition brief offered $100,000 in prizes and invited architects to create "the world's most beautiful office building for the World's Greatest Newspaper."[23] His entry was considered a masterpiece of architectural design, but shockingly, it received only second prize.[24] Louis Sullivan, widely considered the creator of the modern skyscraper, wrote this description of the submission:

> The Finnish master-edifice is not a lonely cry in the wilderness; it is a voice, resonant and rich, ringing amidst the wealth and joy of life. In utterance sublime and melodious, it prophesies a time to come, and not so far away, when the wretched and the yearning, the sordid and the fierce, shall escape the bondage of fixed ideas.[25]

The second prize came with an award of $20,000, which Saarinen used to travel to the United States for the first time. Economic times were difficult in Finland, and America's building construction future seemed much more promising. Soon after he arrived, his wife, Loja, a gifted sculptor, weaver, model maker, and photographer, and their two children, Pipsan and Eero, joined him, and the family took up residence in Evanston, Illinois.[26] In fall 1923 Saarinen was invited by Emil Lorch, dean of the University of Michigan's School of Architecture, to be a guest professor.[27] He and his family moved to Ann Arbor. There, two of his students, Henry Scripps Booth and J. Robert F. Swanson (later to become his son-in-law and partner), introduced him to Henry's father, George G. Booth, publisher of the *Detroit News* and a philanthropist with an interest in education and the arts.[28] Marianne Strengell, a textile designer and weaving professor at Cranbrook, later recalled that Booth had initially proposed a museum, but Saarinen influenced him to consider a school instead:

Mr. Booth wanted to have immortality, I suppose. He had money and he had a beautiful, enormous piece of land in Bloomfield Hills, Michigan, and he thought he would just start a museum. And I think Eliel managed to talk him out of that and say that a living person is more important. "There's lots of museums, and why don't you start a school?"[29]

Thus, the idea was planted to found a new school with a focus on art and craft, and Booth invited Saarinen to prepare designs for the campus. This led to his first architectural work in the United States: the Cranbrook School for Boys in Bloomfield Hills, Michigan, and eventually its Kingswood School for Girls, Institute of Science, and the Academy of Art and Art Museum.[30] Saarinen was elected president of the Cranbrook Academy of Art in 1932 and developed a pioneering graduate program that influenced an emerging generation of designers.[31] Strengell recalled: "He felt what I always felt, too, that it shouldn't just be somebody coming in and sitting down and saying something, you know, year after year after year. He wanted people who were active, who were doing things….That was his philosophy, that people who are teaching should also be doers."[32]

Graduate students in architecture were first accepted in 1931, a year before the academy officially opened, and admitted only if they had prior professional training. They were expected to work on large-scale design problems of their own choosing. Eliel functioned as a critic and visited the studios every day. The emphasis was on studio work, not formal classes.[33] One notable student, Ruth Adler Schnee, recalled:

Eliel and Loja had the graduate students come to the house once a week. And in their living room, Eliel would sit on this very stiff chair….And he always said he was extremely comfortable in that chair, and Loja would sit on a bench…. Her tapestries were hanging from the ceiling, down the wall, across the bench. And we students were draped around the floor. And I have to say, this is really where I learned design philosophy and I learned the discipline that I think has guided me all my life.[34]

top left
Model of Eliel Saarinen's 1925 plan for Cranbrook's Academy of Art and School for Boys, ca. 1925

bottom left
Eliel Saarinen works on a model as students look on, December 1949

right
Cranbrook Academy of Art Design department, Charles Eames at center, Ben Baldwin at far right, April 1940

Executives stand behind a General Motors Technical Center scale model, presented at a luncheon at the Waldorf Astoria hotel in New York on July 24, 1945. Left to right: Charles Kettering, vice president and director of Research; Charles E. Wilson, president; Charles L. McCuen, vice president of Engineering; B. D. Kunkle, vice president; Eero Saarinen, consultant to Saarinen and Swanson; Eliel Saarinen and J. Robert F. Swanson, principals of Saarinen and Swanson; Alfred P. Sloan, board chair; Harley Earl, vice president of Styling (partially obscured); and William J. Davidson, executive engineer. The entire group of buildings on the left are research laboratories; on the right is the administration building. At the far end of the lake is the Styling building; at the upper left is the Engineering building.

Students worked together, focusing on the ideals of the Arts and Crafts movement with an art deco influence. Through this intensely philosophical and collaborative environment, a modern style emerged. Some of the most notable students were Charles Eames, Ray Kaiser Eames, Harry Bertoia, Florence Knoll, and Saarinen's own son, Eero, all of whom would play a prominent role in shaping postwar modernism in the United States. Beginning in the mid-1930s, Eliel Saarinen also ran an independent architecture firm, and it was in this capacity that he came to the attention of the leadership at GM.

Saarinen and Swanson began development on the Technical Center with an agreement to develop a design proposal, which was presented at a regular meeting of the General Motors board of directors on May 7, 1945.[35] The board was shown

> a screen presentation of the presently proposed general plans for the technical center, and…a small model of the architectural layout. The directors were advised that it is planned to provide sufficient facilities so that the Art and Color [sic] Section may have ample space for arranging studios for carrying on their work in the most efficient and effective manner, and the Research Section may have ample opportunity for the development and testing of new devices without the restrictions that necessarily apply in the more congested areas of the city. The chairman stated that tentative estimates indicate this technical center may cost approximately $15,000,000.[36]

The plans were unanimously approved, and the proposal was first presented publicly to a representative group of scientists, educators, engineers, journalists, and industrialists at the "More Jobs through Research" luncheon at New York's Waldorf Astoria hotel on July 24, 1945. GM board chair Alfred Sloan explained the purpose of this campus to those assembled:

This new Technical Center represents long-considered plans of General Motors to expand, at the right time and on a broad scale, its peacetime research, engineering, and development activities and even more progressively pursue its prewar policy of continual product improvement. Thus, to accelerate not only the development of new products through the utilization of new inventions,…the end objective is more and better things at lower prices, thus expanding job opportunities and contributing to an advancing standard of living.…Modern science is the real source of economic progress.…It is to accelerate the progress of scientific advancement that the General Motors Technical Center is dedicated.[37]

The presentation included a complete seven-by-four-foot scale model by James Robert Smith, primary model maker for the Saarinen firm.[38] Models were important design tools in Saarinen's practice; coupled with the expert renderings of the influential and extraordinary architectural delineator Hugh Ferriss, they brought the firm's design visions to life in realistic detail. The renderings—widely published by the design press, including *Architectural Forum*, *Architectural Record*, *Pencil Points*, and *Architect and Engineer*—featured streamlined, expressive forms. *Architectural Forum* lauded the vision: "That architecture here takes a forward leap is due to no straining toward the special or spectacular. General Motors and their architects have managed to translate everyday ordinary industrial buildings—no trimmings, no special shapes—into architectural eloquence."[39]

From the start, GM consciously owned and managed the project's messaging. They published advertisements announcing that it promised "to stimulate opportunities, promote employment and bring about MORE and BETTER THINGS for MORE PEOPLE."[40] This would be a place where GM's researchers, engineers, and stylists would explore the future. The phrase "World of Tomorrow" had first been used as the theme of the 1939 World's Fair in New York, where the popular GM Futurama exhibit envisioned a "suburbanized metropolitan region in the year 1960."[41] Connections between the Futurama exhibit and the Technical Center are overt in many period press releases and other documents, evidencing GM's overall public relations agenda and the broader postwar focus on the future.[42] *Architectural Record* wrote, "The much heralded 'World of Tomorrow' seems a bit less ephemeral with this vision of what one corporation promises in the way of research."[43]

GM leadership used similar messaging when promoting its proposed Technical Center to shareholders in its 1945 annual report: "Here the challenge of the future will be met with the best available scientific equipment and talent." The report also focused on the company's legacy of research and engineering advancements and its policy of "ever-expanding activity in the field of technological improvement," proclaiming that "research stimulates progress."[44] The Technical Center would foment scientific collaboration; seasoned researchers and fresh young minds would converge there to develop ideas and solve problems both new and old, toward the betterment of society.

The philosophy behind the design of the Technical Center was a "desire to build a superlative group of buildings…[that] would have been a credit to the corporation and to the architects."[45] The campus was organized into separate buildings for each section or discipline, as had been directed in 1944 by Sloan. Working with the landscape architect Thomas Dolliver Church, the architects placed buildings around a sunken, irregularly shaped, oblong seven-acre lake. The buildings were connected by parkways and sheltered pedestrian walks over perimeter roadways and surrounded by broad lawns and landscaping.[46]

Presentation drawing by
Hugh Ferriss, 1945

above and opposite
Renderings of GM Technical Center
by Hugh Ferriss, 1945

TO SPEED THE PACE
—and bring you better th

THE BUILDINGS of the Technical Center will face a seven-acre lake. These buildings will be connected by a covered walk and vehicular roadway. Sketched below is the Advanced Engineering Building in which improvements will be quickly made in existing products.

LOCATED ON a major highway leading from Detroit, access to the Center will be through the Administration Building sketched here. A system of modern roadways will provide practical opportunity to study traffic control as well as to make simple road tests of new car developments.

F PROGRESS

os more quickly

A FLOOD OF SUNSHINE will pour into the southern windows of the Research Buildings where experimental work is carried on in such diverse fields as the study of chlorophyl, research into fuels and engine design.

Access roads were at the same lower level as the lake, to keep automobile
and pedestrian traffic and parking out of sight.[47] The Research building was
located north of the lake, Styling to the south, Process Development (or Process
Engineering) northeast, and the Service group and Engineering southeast,
with an eight-story glass and marble administration headquarters building
opposite the main entrance off Mound Road.[48]

The design represented a distinct departure from the previous work of
Eliel Saarinen and Robert Swanson. It bore some resemblance to the streamlined 1939 World's Fair General Motors Futurama pavilion designed by Kahn and
Bel Geddes. (Interestingly, Eero had worked on the pavilion for Bel Geddes.)[49]
Each pavilion had a unique character reflecting the function of the discipline
it housed. Many were rectilinear and featured an upper level with a cantilevered
overhang that created the illusion of floating.[50]

GM's architectural division, Argonaut Realty, sold the existing agricultural
and residential buildings on the property at auction in August 1945, and GM
entered into a formal contract with Saarinen and Swanson on September 19,
1945. Civil, mechanical, electrical, structural engineering, and site development firms were contracted to assist the architects.[51] Construction documents
were completed for site preparation by September 1945, with Hubbell, Roth
& Clark serving as site engineers.[52] Groundbreaking ceremonies were held
during the week of October 25, with Kettering performing the honors—not
with the traditional silver spade but with an eighteen-cubic-yard earth mover.[53]
Site clearing, general grading, installation of water and sewer systems, and
excavation for the planned lake took place from fall 1945 through
summer 1946.[54]

Excavation at the GM Technical
Center site, spring 1946

Up until this time, Eliel's son, Eero, had occupied a limited role in the project, as he had volunteered for service in the Office of Strategic Services (OSS, the precursor to the CIA) in Washington, DC. There he was serving as a consultant to the Special Exhibitions section, producing scale models "to equip the [White House] situation room" and overseeing visual communication.[55] This experience managing projects requiring large-scale organizational thinking equipped him to eventually take on the GMTC and other future projects. Upon Eero's return to Detroit in 1946, he began work as a consultant on the project. Although the basic outlines of the design had been developed, he began preparing proposals that suggested a move toward a more International Style, or Miesian, approach.[56]

When the construction grading and excavation were all but complete, the project was stopped abruptly in October 1946. Several factors led to this decision. At the end of World War II there were significant shortages in building materials, steel in particular. And a new "war" at home was beginning—one that pitted workers against employers. On August 16, 1945, President Harry Truman lifted the wartime wage freeze, announcing that he would maintain price controls but that unions could pursue higher wages. Later that same day the United Automobile Workers and the Congress of Industrial Organizations (UAW-CIO) demanded a 30 percent increase in wages from GM.[57]

The union's position did not proceed from the traditional philosophy of trade unionism at the time. It formed an unprecedented argument that labor was entitled not only to sufficient wages to live on but also to a share in the wealth produced by industry. In other words, it proposed that profits were a legitimate subject of collective bargaining.[58]

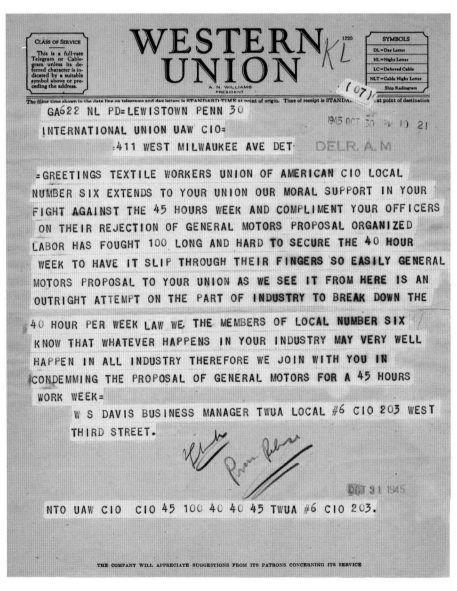

above
UAW-CIO workers on strike picket
GM, December 10, 1945

right
Western Union telegram sent to
the UAW-CIO by the Textile Workers
Union in support of the strike,
October 31, 1945

UAW-CIO lead negotiator Walter Reuther answered GM's plea of inability to pay with a demand that the corporation "open its books." After six weeks of fruitless bargaining, GM made the union a counteroffer: a ten-cent-per-hour wage increase; an increase in the hours in the work week (see telegram); and the union's cooperation with GM in seeking government approval for a corresponding 10 percent price hike on new cars. The union rejected this offer, and on November 21, 1945, approximately 180,000 workers walked out.[59]

In December President Truman declared the strike a major obstacle holding up the nation's reconversion program. When he appointed a fact-finding board that demanded to see the company's books, the GM bargainers walked out.[60] Three months later, after 113 days of the strike, Charles Wilson, president of GM, and Phillip Murray, president of the CIO, signed a historic two-year contract calling for an 18.5 percent wage hike and the elimination of annual economic negotiations with the acceptance of a longer-term contract. The agreement introduced a new wage formula that provided for a cost-of-living allowance and laid the basis for escalator clauses that allowed for changes based on factors beyond the control of either party, such as inflation, and an annual improvement factor based on increased efficiency resulting from advancing technology.[61] It was a long and costly strike, ushering in a new era in American labor relations.

In March 1946 GM halted further work on the Technical Center in Warren, due in part to the crippling strike, and focused its resources and capital on expanding automotive production capabilities to meet the intense postwar consumer demand for automobiles.[62] Strike costs and other pressures from within the company and without had led GM leadership to conclude that a significant reduction of $100 million in its postwar program was necessary.[63] In light of this decision, the Technical Center project, as well as a proposed Chevrolet Light Car program, were defunded and canceled.[64] The contract with Saarinen and Swanson was ended and a settlement made with them in October that included the termination of their services and those of their consultants. But even as the overall Technical Center undertaking was on hold, GM's Engineering staff continued work on detailing the specific building requirements for their own section.[65]

CHAPTER THREE

Eero Saarinen

On July 29, 1948, General Motors' Administration Committee met and discussed reviving the Technical Center project. Alfred Sloan explained to those gathered that

> he had discussed this matter with various officials of the Corporation and that revival of the plans, for construction of one unit at a time, may be considered. He stated that he is requesting Executive Vice President O. E. Hunt to assume jurisdiction in connection with revival of the plans for construction of the Technical Center and has asked Mr. Hunt to survey the matter and to submit his recommendations to the Committee for consideration at a later meeting.[1]

It no doubt seemed natural to Sloan that Ormond E. Hunt would take responsibility for the revival of the plans, as it was his Engineering staff that had continued to plan for new facilities while the Technical Center project was on hold. A little more than five months after this meeting and more than two years after the contract with Saarinen and Swanson was terminated, GM was ready to resume the undertaking.

In the intervening years, many things had changed in the Saarinen office. Eero had returned from Washington, DC, in 1946 to become a partner at the firm, which was renamed Saarinen, Swanson & Saarinen.[2] It didn't last long, however, as Robert Swanson (Eero's brother-in-law) became fed up with "Eero's consistent refusals to meet design deadlines, which significantly eroded the firm's profits…or as one old-timer put it, 'We'll make money on Eliel's job and lose it on Eero's.'"[3] Swanson left and started his own firm, and father and son formed their partnership as Saarinen, Saarinen and Associates. Not long after, Eliel's health began to decline and Eero's role began to expand. This was the juncture at which GM came back to reengage the firm.

GM had a bit of a dilemma, as they had been dealing before with Saarinen and Swanson. To continue with the Saarinens' firm would mean trusting the thirty-eight-year-old Eero, who had limited experience with large-scale projects, as the lead architect. There was some discussion within the GM leadership of considering other architects. Charles Kettering, who had remained a consultant to the company and a major influence on its direction despite having retired in 1947, still favored Albert Kahn.[4] But Harley Earl was steadfast in his support of Eero. He convinced GM leadership to take a calculated risk on the relatively unknown architect with the assurance that Eliel would still be involved to a certain extent. Thus, the career of Eero Saarinen was definitively launched with a commission that would prove influential to corporate architecture in the postwar United States, setting him up for numerous large projects to come.

Eero Saarinen (1910–1961) was born into a truly extraordinary artistic environment and spent his childhood in an atmosphere of disciplined architectural study, guided by his profound and close relationship with his father. He literally learned at his father's knee.[5] As a boy in Finland, his parents' home was a cultural nexus for an elite Finnish and European cadre of musicians, composers, artists, and other creative individuals. A respect for the harmony and interconnectedness of nature, art, life, and humanity was an inherent part of his upbringing. In Eero's words:

> I was a very lucky little boy. We, as a family, lived in Finland until I was twelve years old. My father had his architectural studio right in the house. The whole family would sit at one end of the studio. As a child, I would always draw and I happened to be good at it. Therefore, I got more attention from drawing than anything else. They made me draw more and more. Later, [Géza] Maróti, a Hungarian sculptor who was a friend of my parents, took me in hand and made me really work at it. He made me draw from nature and study anatomy and he would make me do things over and over. I was only praised if what I did was good, not the way children are praised today for anything they do.[6]

This search for form at such a young age was rooted in the philosophical fascination that Eliel brought to his own work, with a structured methodology for organized visual thought and open problem solving. When Eero was a teenager, his father began assigning him jobs, for instance designing decorative elements for the Cranbrook complex. From the late 1930s, Eero was encouraged to enter competitions and used these opportunities to develop his design approach and presentation skills.[7]

top
Eliel and Eero Saarinen, ca. 1918

bottom
Detail of drawing of Cranbrook dormitories made by an eighteen-year-old Eero Saarinen, 1929

Eero also had a deep connection with his mother, Loja, a textile artist and sculptor who founded the weaving department at Cranbrook. She nurtured his creative life, and he later claimed that it was she who influenced him most to pursue an artistic career.[8] Eero first studied sculpture for one year at the Académie de la Grande Chaumière in Paris before enrolling at the Yale School of Architecture.[9] When he graduated from Yale in 1934, he won the Charles Ormrod Matcham Fellowship. This prize supported two years of travel throughout Europe and the Middle East, during which time he absorbed architecture and met architects. He took a position at the architectural firm of his uncle, Jarl Eklund, before returning to Cranbrook in the summer of 1936.[10]

Eero came back both to begin work as a consultant at his father's practice and to teach at Cranbrook, the scene of a burgeoning cultural movement. A group of amazingly talented and forward-thinking individuals had arrived there to study with Eliel. According to Timo Tuomi, head of research at the Museum of Finnish Architecture, "Because of [Eliel's] connections, he got all the big names of the time to come and lecture to Cranbrook....There was Alvar Aalto, Le Corbusier...everybody who was somebody then knew Eliel, and he was the guy who got them to Cranbrook."[11]

Eliel was not the only attraction. The Cranbrook Academy of Art, which officially opened in 1932, had been reorganized as a new and vibrant residential community and had begun to attract highly creative and interesting artists, designers, and craftspeople as both faculty and students. In many ways it was the US equivalent of the Bauhaus in Germany: both schools emphasized the interconnectedness of the various art and design disciplines and encouraged students to explore new forms and languages for design in the twentieth century. The difference was that there was no formula or visual edict at Cranbrook, as there clearly was in the Bauhaus.[12] It was a quieter, more humane approach that encouraged a laboratory environment for the exploration of form, process, and materials. The academy's 1932 catalog described this curriculum as a "working place for creative art."[13] Lilian Swann Saarinen, Eero's first wife, recalled her impressions as a new student:

left
Loja Saarinen, 1932

right
Lilian Swann Saarinen, 1941

Eliel's ideas fitted [George] Booth's idea of a great big barn where a whole lot of artists got together and they all shared their talents. One would be reading in one corner, and one would be doing metal in another corner, and one would be doing drawing and sculpting and so forth. There'd be groups, and they'd all be working together and help each other. And that's exactly what Eliel believed, and that's exactly what Cranbrook had.[14]

The names of many of the people associated with Cranbrook became synonymous with midcentury modern design in the United States: Marianne Strengell, Eszter Haraszty, Loja Saarinen, Maija Grotell, Ruth Adler Schnee, Hans Knoll, Florence Knoll, Wallace Mitchell, Zoltan L. Sepeshy, Harry Bertoia, Edmund Bacon, Harry Weese, Charles Eames, Ray Kaiser Eames, Ralph Rapson. It was a rich environment for interdisciplinary collaboration, experimentation, and invention. Eero's closest and most important relationship was with Charles Eames, which led to a series of highly progressive and prize-winning furniture designs for the 1939 "Organic Design in Home Furnishings" competition and 1940 exhibition hosted by the Museum of Modern Art in New York. Subsequently he produced a number of iconic furniture designs for Knoll International. Joseph Lacy, who was initially hired as a manager at Saarinen's firm and ultimately became a partner, recalled:

> Eero's first chair design started with a small sheet of aluminum that he cut and bent into shapes until he was satisfied with the design. The shape was curved but all were simple curves, not compound. His furniture models were produced in our model shop. Eero employed a designer to carry out his designs at full size. His first chair, after the final model was finished, was produced by Knoll Associates, a furniture manufacturer in New York. Eero knew Hans Knoll as he was married to a Cranbrook girl who was also a furniture designer. Eero's first chair was very successful and, because of its shape, it became known as the "Womb" chair. I told Eero I would love to have one but I had figured that if I put a meter on my favorite chair at home and put a quarter in it each time I sat down it would be years before I would have enough to buy the chair.[15]

These early collaborative experiments with Eames, as well as his entries and awards in furniture design competitions, were the beginnings of Eero setting out in his own direction—a different path than the one his father had walked.[16]

Concurrently, Eliel and Eero began to collaborate on projects, and their unique relationship progressed from father-son and mentor-student to a comfortable partnership of collegial respect. Eero worked on the original Saarinen and Swanson proposal for the GM Technical Center, as well as on other commissions.[17] By many accounts, "each benefited from the expertise, inspiration, and talent of the other."[18]

On December 3, 1948, a new contract to restart the Technical Center project was executed between General Motors and Saarinen, Saarinen and Associates. Smith, Hinchman & Grylls, Inc. (SH&G) was designated as "architect-engineer," functioning as co-architects in design and development.[19] With this agreement, Eero was handed the opportunity of a lifetime as the design lead for this vast project—one of the largest architectural commissions of the twentieth century. Lacy recalled:

top
Eero Saarinen, Charles Eames, and Warren Booth at the opening of the 1939 Cranbrook Academy of Art faculty exhibition, December 1939

bottom
Composite photograph of a chair designed by Charles Eames and Eero Saarinen for *Organic Design in Home Furnishings*, a competition and exhibition hosted by the Museum of Modern Art, New York, May 1941

In 1948, the General Motors Technical Center project came to life. At their invitation, we met with the GM representatives. I was in on that meeting which was held at Eliel's house. First, they asked if we would be interested in going ahead with the project. Naturally we wanted to complete the project and we said so. However, Eero told them there would be one condition and that was to revise the original design. He told them that the original design was too spread out and it should be changed to bring the buildings closer together. Also, he explained that because of inflation and the necessity to modify the design to stay within the budget, a new approach was desirable. They agreed and so we proceeded with a new design. Because so much site work [e.g., excavation] and underground utilities were done earlier, there were some restrictions and the new scheme had to be somewhat similar to the first one but it placed the buildings closer together in a tighter perimeter.[20]

Eero's revised concept aligned more with his own aesthetic vision, which embodied an American interpretation of the International Style:

When the General Motors people first came to my father for the General Motors Technical Center they probably thought and imagined in their mind that they would get something like Cranbrook. But the problem was a different one. The whole spirit of what they stood for was a different one. The time was a different one.[21]

His father offered critical support for this radical change in direction and worked closely with Eero during its early development.[22]

Eero felt that the original design, dominated by gray concrete, should have more of a visual relationship with the materials of the automobile itself, such as metal and glass. GM gave Eero a great deal of freedom to develop this new aesthetic for the campus; however, they also expected solutions for many engineering and design problems that had become apparent in the analysis of the first proposal. For instance, one important requirement was that the built spaces should easily accommodate change and modification.[23]

In a letter to Astrid Sampe, a colleague and textile designer from Sweden, Eero described his role:

Proposed site plan by Saarinen, Saarinen and Associates, undated

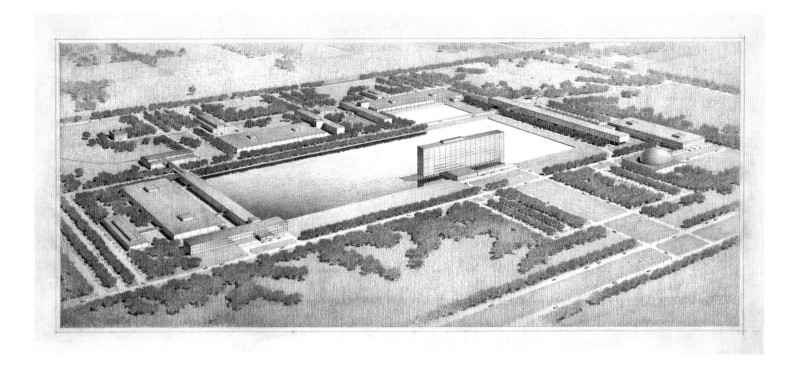

It is seldom that one gets a chance to redesign a thing that big and get a chance
to correct all one's mistakes and make a whole new set of mistakes....Actually
I am quite enthusiastic about the new plan. I think it will be really good—and as
you know I don't often praise our own work. The buildings are going to be very very
simple. The whole thing will look like a small city of factory buildings in a park and in
the middle of the park is a large man-made lake. The whole group will, when built,
cost about 25 to 30 million dollars.[24]

In the end, Eero's estimation was off by a factor of nearly six: the project
cost upward of $150 million by the time it was finished in 1956.

Eero submitted his first drawings for the new design shortly after receiving
the contract. By February 2, 1949, the initial scale models had been completed
and revealed to GM leadership.[25] Some elements of the original concept were
carried over, namely buildings and roadways surrounding a rectangular lake with
a water tower and a large administration building. But the lake was now squared
off to a rectangle of 1,780 by 560 feet and spanned approximately twenty-two
acres—an almost threefold increase.[26] The buildings were horizontal, simplified
rectangular structures; a large, vertical administration building rose out of the
lake. In the end, that building was removed and replaced with a huge fountain
115 feet wide by 50 feet high to retain the "vertical focal point" with a massive
wall of moving water. The low buildings around the lake reinforced the overall
landscape design by Thomas Dolliver Church, which accentuated the horizontal
feeling of the campus.

Eero's plan was quite simple, oriented north to south and surrounding
the lake on three sides. Five major buildings housed the various disciplines:
Research (north); Styling (south); Process Development, later known as
Manufacturing A (northeast); the Service group, later redesignated Manufacturing B and C (east, south of Manufacturing A); and Engineering (southeast).
The Central Restaurant (east) was a separate structure set back between
Manufacturing A and Engineering. A main gatehouse was placed at the entrance
on the west side of the campus; an additional gatehouse was located to the
south. Main roads bordered the lake, except in front of Research; the flat
lawn areas, lake, pools, and parking lots were a series of rectangular planes.

SAARINEN SAARINEN AND ASSOCIATES [1948] **1.**

ELIEL SAARINEN F.A.I.A.
EERO SAARINEN A.I.A.
JOSEPH N. LACY A.I.A.
J. HENDERSON BARR

Kära lilla Sumpe

Tack så jätteligt mycket för boken — ennu
jag ej läst den mera utom aldeles den förs.
delen — snart kommer jag att läsa den och sen
skriver jag igen — mitt intryck är vad jag h
sett är mycket mycket bra. Formatet är br
pärmen är. Rätt charactär bildarna äro väldi
bra och valda och att börja med en
konversation mellan dig och Vera Diurson är
också att bra och enkelt sett att få fram
era två synpunkter. Anyway, Congratulation
for what looks like a very good job. It really
looks wonderfull.

I am again sitting in a plane — this time
to going to Minneapolis, Minnesota — on the
way back I will be reading your book but this
trip is reserved for writing to you.
For the last three months (except for a week
skiing) I have been completly absorbed in work
that is why I will write about work first. We
have a terrifying amount of work to do. The most
interesting of our diffent projects and also the
biggest is a Research Center for General Motors
I may have told you a bit about it earlier

ARCHITECTS · BLOOMFIELD HILLS, MICHIGAN · PHONE BIRMINGHAM 5037

SAARINEN SAARINEN AND ASSOCIATES **2.**

ELIEL SAARINEN F.A.I.A.
EERO SAARINEN A.I.A.
JOSEPH N. LACY A.I.A.
J. HENDERSON BARR

We were working on it earlier but the project was
discontinued about two years ago — now - 3
months ago they have decided to go ahead again
but with a new plan entarly — It is very seldome
that one gets a chance to redesign a thing that
big and get a chance to correct all ones mistakes
and make a whole new set of mistakes.
— actually I am quite enthusiastic about
the new plan I think it will be really
good — and as you know I don't often
praise our own work. the buildings are going
to be very very simple the whole thing will look
like a small city of factory buildings in a
park and in the middle of the park is a
large man made lake. the whole group
will when built cost about 25 to 30 million
dollus what is that in crowns must be
something like 140 000 000 crowns — it is
about ½ of the United Nations that Harrison
is doing — When you come the next time
to this part of the world I will show you
the real thing

ARCHITECTS · BLOOMFIELD HILLS, MICHIGAN · PHONE BIRMINGHAM 5037

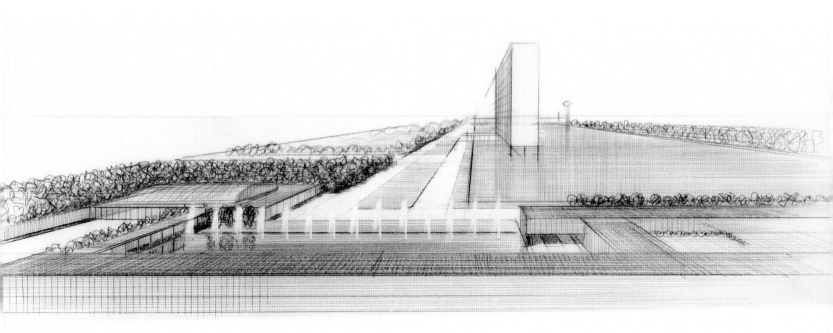

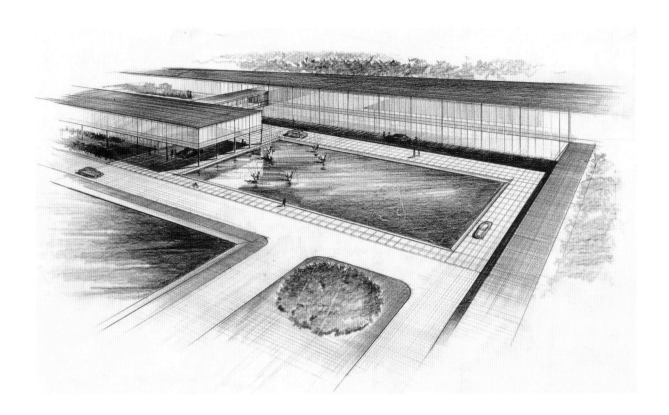

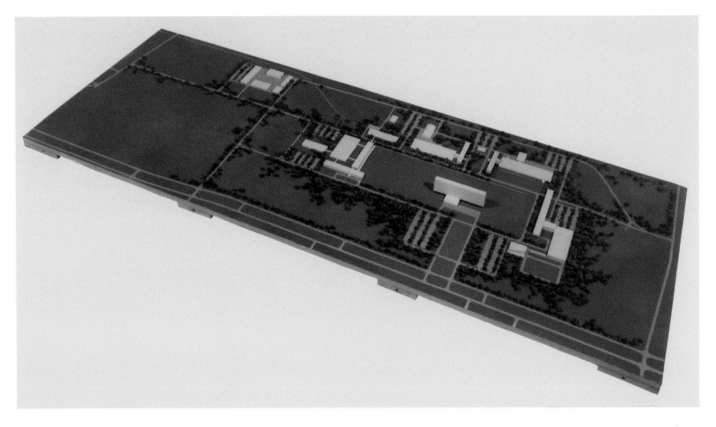

top
Proposed site plan, undated

bottom
Model of Engineering buildings by
Saarinen, Saarinen and Associates as
of February 1, 1949, before changes
to Research and Service section
buildings, as viewed from Mound
Road, April 19, 1949

opposite top
Rendering of the GM Research
laboratories administration
building, 1950

opposite center
Perspective of Research metallurgical
building, January 5, 1949

opposite bottom left
Rendering by Saarinen and
Associates of fountain outside
Styling building, ca. 1951

opposite bottom right
Rendering by Saarinen and
Associates of central fountain,
ca. 1951

61 CHAPTER THREE: EERO SAARINEN

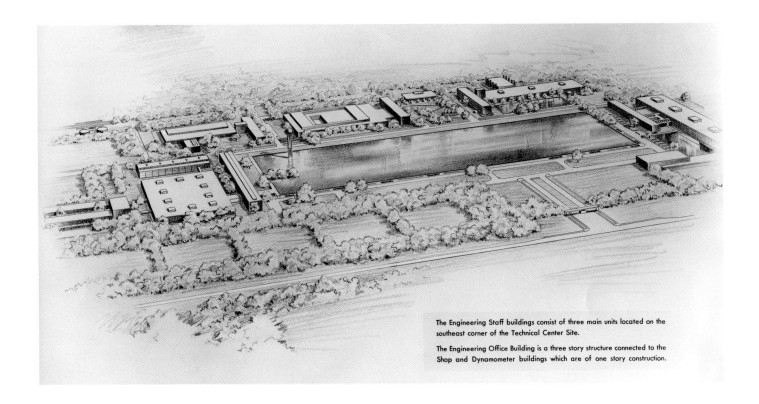

The Engineering Staff buildings consist of three main units located on the southeast corner of the Technical Center Site.

The Engineering Office Building is a three story structure connected to the Shop and Dynamometer buildings which are of one story construction.

Trees were planted in groupings, and a forest acted as a buffer from the outside, which provided an element of security to the complex but was also meant to "give the lawns the effect of clearings."[27] A large water tower punctuated the lake, complementing the vertical water feature. A rail line separated the original campus from undeveloped GM property to the east. Eero expressed his concept:

> The architecture attempts to find its eloquence out of a consistent and logical development of its industrial character. It has been said that in these buildings I was very much influenced by Mies. But this architecture really carries forward the tradition of the American factory buildings which had its roots in the Middle West in the early automobile factories of Albert Kahn. Certainly, the scale of building, the rigorous grid, and the stark simplicity of forms of the General Motors Technical Center recall Kahn's designs for Highland Park and River Rouge.[28]

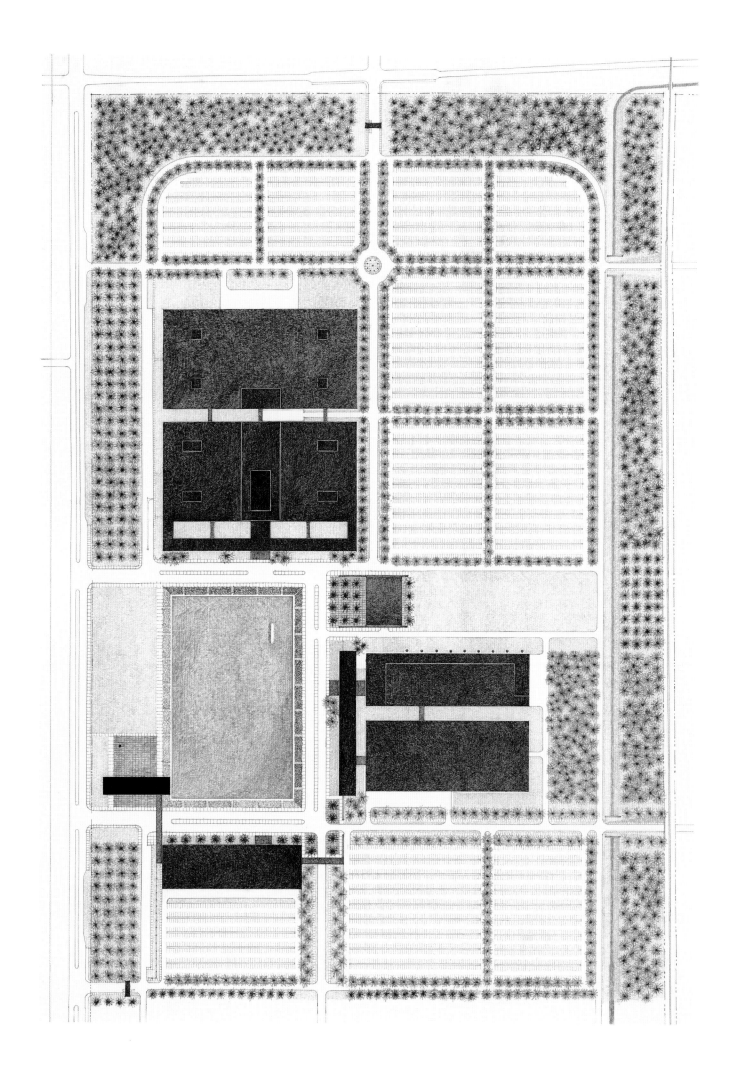

Architectural Forum published an article on the preliminary design in July 1949, which announced Eero Saarinen as the lead architect. This was the beginning of the press's love affair with the project. Before construction had even begun, the magazine described the architecture as

> taking a forward leap, due to no straining toward the special or spectacular that managed to translate everyday ordinary industrial buildings—no trimmings, no special shapes—into architectural eloquence. Here is an object lesson in what architecture can do on realistic grounds. The achievement is one of thoughtfulness instead of expenditure, of analysis instead of fancy.[29]

It is likely that Kettering and du Pont's concerns may have been alleviated by this assessment, which at the same time satisfied Earl's desire for a significant aesthetic achievement. Since the Saarinen office was relatively small, Eero needed to quickly form a team to manage and execute this massive project. He sought out some of the very best talent of the times, as Lacy described:

> Eero had a penchant for locating promising young designers to add to our staff. He knew several Deans of the best architectural schools and he would call them for the names of their best and most talented students in the graduating class and then attempt to lure them to work for us. He managed to add several to our staff.... Eero's reputation became well known and young designers came to apply for jobs in order to work under Eero. Our office got to be sort of like a graduate school for them. Most of them stayed for two or three years and then moved on to other offices to broaden their experience.[30]

The most important hire was Kevin Roche. Roche had been deeply influenced by a brief but important study experience with Ludwig Mies van der Rohe at the Illinois Institute of Technology in Chicago, then had made his way to New York before a chance meeting with Eero, who hired him on the spot.[31] Lacy described him:

> He was a native of Ireland and had gotten his architectural education there. Eero assigned him to do a drawing for a competition and when it was finished Eero said the man couldn't draw. Later on, the young man, Kevin Roche, turned out to be a brilliant designer and was Eero's right hand man.[32]

Eero Saarinen, Kevin Roche, and Frederick T. Kubitz working on the TWA terminal, ca. 1955

When Roche arrived in Detroit in 1950, there were only ten people working in the Saarinen office, and he reported directly to Warren Platner. John Dinkeloo, an architect and Roche's future partner, arrived two weeks later and built up the production group. Bonus agreements were negotiated with two partners and critical members of Eero's team: J. Henderson Barr, an architect and extraordinary delineator, and Lacy, an architect and business manager for the Saarinen office. These bonus agreements were meant to incentivize the completion of design drawings to meet the project's schedule. Once the drawings were done, they were sent to Smith, Hinchman & Grylls, the architect-engineer, to produce the construction documents.[33] The Saarinen firm paid them for services such as "supervision, site plan, preliminary design, working drawings & specifications, resident engineers."[34] Minoru Yamasaki was the head of design at SH&G and later designed the World Trade Center in New York. There was a great deal of respect and trust between Saarinen and Yamasaki.[35] The outside consultants to the Saarinen firm, including many that Eero knew from his days at Cranbrook, were a testament to the depth of the design community centered in the Detroit area at the time. Kevin Roche recalled, "I didn't want to go to Detroit. I thought it was the end of the world, but it really was the center of architectural development at that moment in time in America. The idea of design teams originated in Detroit."[36]

Eero had embraced the use of models from a young age as a method of visual evaluation; they were an essential component of the Saarinen design process. In Lacy's words:

> Eero developed many rough sketches of an idea and then carried them into three-dimensional models. It seemed to me that he was unsure in two-dimensional drawings and went on to test them in model form. This may have been the result of his early venture into sculpture. For a short time in his early career he leaned toward that art form.[37]

James Robert Smith was the primary model maker for eighteen years at the Saarinen office. George Moon recalled the presentation of the Engineering model, which detailed the first building on the site to be constructed:

> To achieve this ten-foot model on time, the staff divided into two groups...one to do the building, itself, the other to achieve the plot, with roads, grading, planting, etc. About an hour before the actual presentation, the model had been taken to the General Motors Building in Detroit and set up in a conference room. This was a highly-detailed model with lighting and a great deal of interior partitioning and furnishings. The group began to set the model up, first laying down the base, then setting the building down on its appointed marks. But, something was wrong. The building overlapped the road, walkways and curbing, by almost six inches. A crisis! James Robert came to the rescue. He took his model saw and carefully cut the building twice, removing a section large enough to have the building sit properly on the plot. It was set down and put together, and no one could tell what was done. The General Motors people came in and loved what they saw. In fact, Eero and his staff had prepared a considerable number of drawings to show all kinds of plans, elevations and details. But the client never looked at them. The model was their focus, and...people are always impressed with a beautiful model. No one noticed the drawings, no one wanted to study those. No one saw the model was actually not correct in length. It made the impression. It sold itself. After that approval meeting, the Saarinen people rushed to recheck the drawings, and they found that the civil engineering drawings were in error. An on-site inspection showed that, true to the civil drawings, the side road was mis-located and about to be paved some forty feet in error.[38]

Eero understood the importance of visual communication for both his team of collaborators and the client: elaborate mock-ups streamlined the design and approval process. The Saarinen office also relied on three-dimensional models to support iterative decision making.[39] The overall placement of the Technical Center's buildings remained fairly consistent, but many iterations of the campus layout were developed and evaluated with scale models. Thirty models of the water tower were designed and built before the final selection, and the shape of the Styling auditorium changed numerous times, as did the vertical elements in the lake.[40] Charles Eames described

above
Scale models of stairs, ca. 1955

overleaf
Architectural scale model of the
Styling building, January 26, 1950

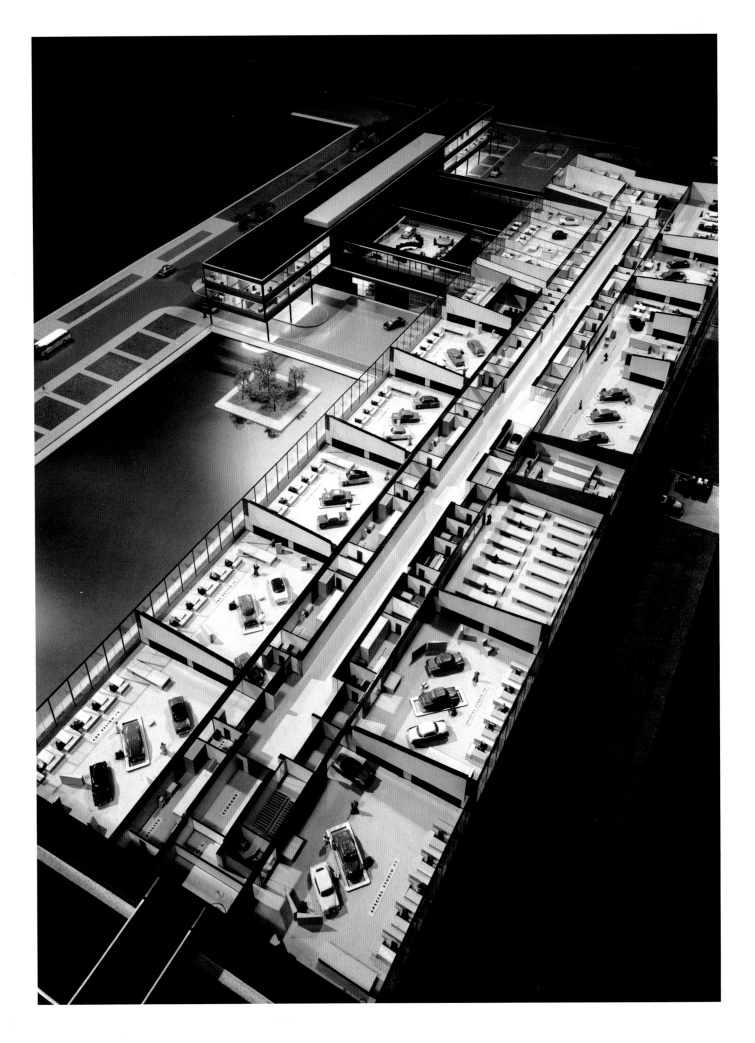

opposite

Architectural scale model of the
Styling building, January 26, 1950

top

Architectural scale model
of the Research laboratories,
January 26, 1950

bottom

Charles L. McCuen, Harlow Curtice,
and Eero Saarinen, October 23, 1950

Eero's fondness for testing by models, both abstract and concrete; innovative building elements were tested at full scale, in real conditions, over time. Energy and experience from each stage of construction were fed back to the successive ones, to upgrade the details and materials.…By the time the center was completed, Eero had become a master of the feedback principle; he had found confirmation of his natural commitment to systems.[41]

Models at various scales, including full-size mock-ups of the exterior curtain wall, were set up at the GM Proving Grounds to test the materials and proportions of the metal-clad wall. Two full-size rooms were set up to test the modular ceiling system with integrated HVAC systems, which introduced plastic panels for the diffusion of light.[42] This appears to be one area where Eero may have been influenced by the association with his client, GM. He was said to have "studied and documented the step-by-step method by which automobile prototypes were subjected to cycles of research and input, learning from the design process of engineers and stylists."[43] A 1951 *Architectural Forum* article noted: "Everything was tested for months in full scale mockups as if it had been the 1955 Buick under design—a procedure as distant as the moon from customary building techniques."[44]

However, the influence has not been substantiated completely; Kevin Roche, who acted as the lead architect on the project under Eero, does not recall much influence coming from GM Styling's model making. In his experience, the car studios were highly controlled environments, not open for the architects to review their processes. Roche supported the use of models at the Saarinen office from the beginning of his tenure there. Eero was an excellent draftsman and could draw the most complicated idea with ease, but he relied on Roche to execute the three-dimensional expression of his drawings as models. He preferred this process for their office and client reviews, to allow for a more focused evaluation of ideas and to permit changes to be made quickly. It also provided a fast and effective way to communicate with the various

top
Early model of Styling auditorium,
ca. 1947–50

center left, center right, and bottom
Completed models of Styling
auditorium, ca. 1955

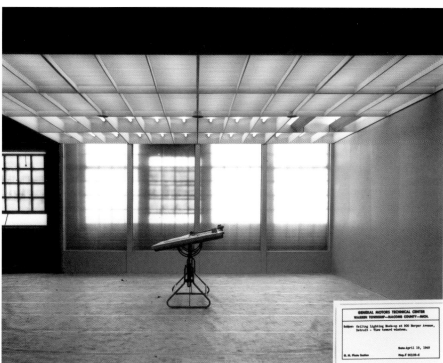

top
Full-scale mock-up of curtain
wall, ca. 1947–50

bottom
Ceiling lighting mock-up at
900 Harper Avenue, Detroit,
April 21, 1949

external collaborators. In Roche's words: "It stopped a lot of arguing about what he was trying to do here....You do a model and it's done. You either like it or you don't like it. I had always liked to do models....I would say that we were the first modern office to use models in modern buildings....It was an essential design tool in those days."[45]

The Saarinen firm worked with many external design firms and individual design consultants, such as Alexander Girard and Ruth Adler Schnee.[46] GM Styling had a significant role with respect to interiors and furniture specification throughout the campus, in particular at the Styling building itself.[47] The Architecture and Interiors group within the Industrial Design department at Styling collaborated with the Saarinen firm and took on the interior design of many spaces completely. Other divisions at GM provided support and research for technical advances that resulted in such innovations as the neoprene gaskets for sealing windows, sandwich-panel insulated walls, special glazes for the bricks, and luminous ceiling panels.[48] Eero brought in the well-known modernist landscape architect Thomas Dolliver Church to work as a consultant in collaboration with Edward Eichstedt, a local landscape architect from Detroit, who supervised the implementation of Church's design.[49] Argonaut Realty, the architectural division at GM, handled construction supervision and designed some specialty technical operations such as a wind tunnel.[50]

The commitment to collaboration in Eero's office no doubt had its beginnings in the Cranbrook environment that his father had created. Eero understood and embraced the role of society and the client as key to developing meaningful solutions; in 1953 he wrote about the role of the client: "He must be part of and understand our civilization. At the same time, he is not just a mirror; he is also a co-creator and must have the strength and urge to produce form, not compromise."[51]

On May 16, 1949, Bryant & Detwiler Company was awarded the contract as the general contractor to execute construction. Detailed drawings for the Engineering building were completed in July 1949, and the excavation of the Technical Center campus was about to begin.[52]

above
Kevin Roche and Eero Saarinen,
1950s

opposite top
Architectural scale model of the
GM Technical Center, May 9, 1955

opposite bottom
Scale model illustrating Styling
auditorium lighting, ca. 1945–46

CHAPTER FOUR

Construction

The GM Technical Center project officially restarted with a press announcement issued Sunday, May 22, 1949:

> Construction of the General Motors Technical Center on the 350-acre site at Mound and Twelve-Mile roads north of Detroit will begin the middle of June, C. E. Wilson, President of General Motors, announced today. The announcement was made in connection with the award of the construction contract to Bryant and Detwiler Company, Detroit. Project architects are Saarinen Saarinen and Associates, Bloomfield Hills, Mich., and the architect-engineers are Smith, Hinchman & Grylls, Inc., Detroit....Architecturally, the buildings will be of unique design, both modern and functional in concept.[1]

Excavation began on July 11, a few weeks later than expected. Minoru Yamasaki was the head of design at Smith, Hinchman & Grylls (SH&G) and a friend and colleague of Eero, which was an important factor in the firm's selection. Joseph Lacy from the Saarinen office recalled:

> We decided to associate with a firm that had a large production staff to do the final working drawings and engineering on the Tech Center rather than build up a staff of our own to do everything in our office. So, we associated with Smith, Hinchman and Grylls in Detroit to do working drawings, specifications and engineering. It turned out to be a very good choice. We turned out complete design drawings for them to work from. A few of their men came into our office to do design drawings under our direction so they would be familiar with the project and could follow through when they returned to their office.[2]

SH&G set up a separate office in the Guardian Building in Detroit, and eventually more than 125 of the firm's architects, engineers, and draftspeople were working there on the Technical Center project.[3] Bryant & Detwiler of Detroit established a field office at the construction site on June 22, 1949. Excavation work was subcontracted in July, and excavation began on the Engineering shop building with an estimated occupancy date of late summer 1950.[4]

Recall that the GM Engineering staff had continued to work on defining their needs and requirements even when the initial project had stopped, so they were able to communicate their wishes to the design team right away, speeding things along. Research staff had done up-front work as well, but the complexities of their discipline required more time to develop plans than was initially allotted. It was a balancing act to design buildings that provided for specific functional needs and at the same time adhered to the overall

opposite
General Motors executives at Research building groundbreaking. Left to right: Harlow H. Curtice, executive vice president in charge of staff activities; Charles E. Wilson, president; Charles L. McCuen, vice president of Research; Charles Kettering, director and former vice president of Research; Charles A. Chayne, vice president of Engineering, May 2, 1952

above
View of the GM Technical Center construction site from Mound Road, May 20, 1954

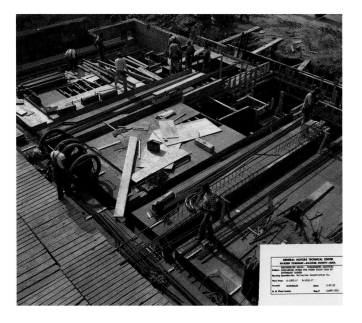

TITLE: Electroplating area showing installation of acid resistant brick floor.　VIEW TOWARD: SE　FROM: First Floor Process Bldg.　DATE: 4-1-53　NEG.# X2308-478

top left
Erection of steel framework for
the Research laboratories building,
December 17, 1952

top right
Slab construction on the
Engineering group Dynamometer
building, May 27, 1955

bottom
Construction on the Process
Development building: electroplating
area showing installation of acid-
resistant brick floor, April 1, 1953

aesthetic that the Saarinen firm had defined.[5] Rising construction costs,
modifications, and redesign work also contributed to this complexity.

The campus plan consisted of building groups devoted to the four
technical disciplines—Engineering, Research, Styling, and Process
Development—and the Service organization, which managed the operations
of the campus. In addition, a stand-alone building housed a central restaurant.
Each of these staff organizations had its own group of buildings, which
included administrative office and technical shop buildings as well as special-
use buildings such as the Dynamometer buildings, all designed as
asymmetrical, flat-roofed structures:

RESEARCH (administration, offices and laboratories, manufacturing, metallurgy, engineering, fuel blending) is where GM looked to the future with long-range projects and studies involving the mechanical arts and basic sciences of chemistry, metallurgy, physics, medicine, and electronics.[6]

ENGINEERING (administration, shop, dynamometer, gasoline blending) specialized in development work on automotive engines, suspensions, automatic transmissions, body structures, and military vehicles and components. Many of the architectural elements of the Engineering buildings were prototypical applications, since it was the first building group to be constructed.[7] For instance, the gasketing material used for sealing the curtain wall failed in the initial tests, but a collaborative effort with GM's Inland Manufacturing division adapted a material used for sealing automobile windshields, which proved successful and ultimately was used for the rest of the campus.

PROCESS DEVELOPMENT (administration, shop/foundry) functioned as a bridge by translating the discoveries of Research into processes that would improve manufacturing techniques and promote quality, efficiency, and reduced costs.[8]

STYLING (administration, studios, fabrication, garage, auditorium with outdoor display yard) was involved with automotive design for each of GM's domestic divisions—Chevrolet, Pontiac, Oldsmobile, Buick, Cadillac, and GMC Truck & Coach—as well as global brands Opel, Vauxhall, and Holden.[9] Also included were design studios for Frigidaire and other nonautomotive divisions, as well as a display group that developed exhibits such as the Parade of Progress and the GM Motorama. It was the largest industrial design center built in its time.[10]

SERVICE (administration, garage and shops, powerhouse, restaurant) operated and maintained the facilities and services of the Technical Center campus, including utilities, communications, medical staff, food, personnel, roads, and landscaping. The Central Restaurant, a stand-alone structure, is between the administration buildings of Engineering and Process Development. Positioned directly across the lake from the main entrance, a courtyard leads to this one-story building. It was designed to serve the entire campus and provide a relaxed, pedestrian-friendly environment.[11]

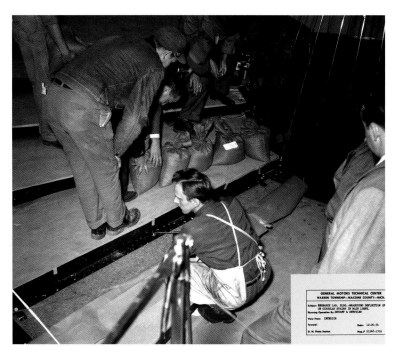

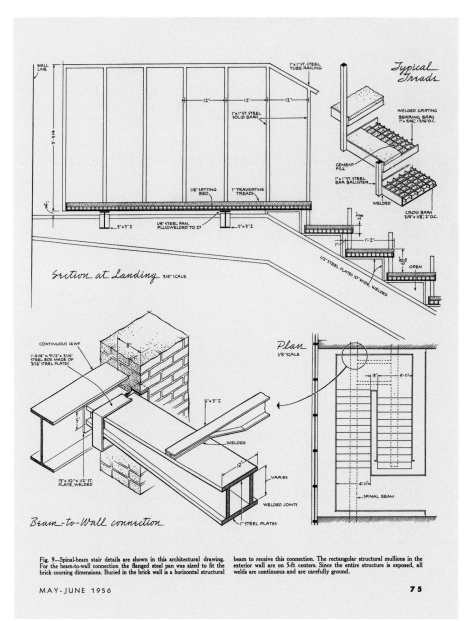

top left
Detail view of lobby staircase tread
in the Styling administration building,
May 21, 2013

top right
Engineering and adjusting the spiral
staircase in the lobby of the Research
administration building, December
20, 1954

bottom
Page from *General Motors
Engineering Journal*, with illustrations
showing the spinal-beam steel
structure of the Service section stairs,
May–June 1956

Fig. 9—Spinal-beam stair details are shown in this architectural drawing. For the beam-to-wall connection the flanged steel pan was sized to fit the brick coursing dimensions. Buried in the brick wall is a horizontal structural beam to receive this connection. The rectangular structural mullions in the exterior wall are on 5-ft centers. Since the entire structure is exposed, all welds are continuous and are carefully ground.

MAY-JUNE 1956

75

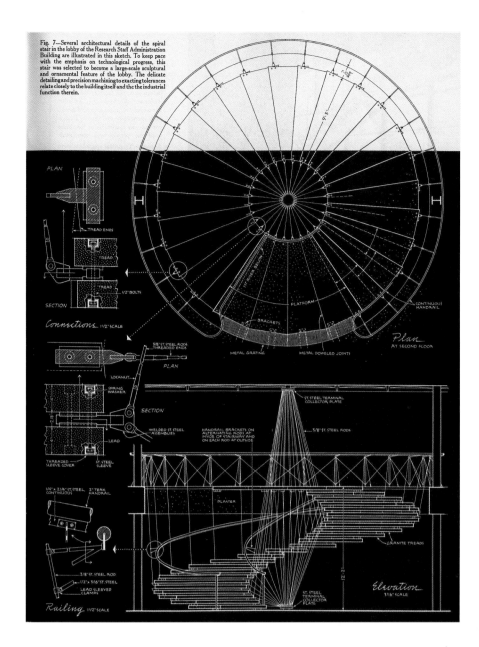

According to Eero:

> Each of the staff organizations prides itself on its own individuality and its range of activities. Each wanted its own "personality." We tried to answer this desire architecturally in the main lobby of each of the five groups. In four of these, the visual climax to the lobby is the main staircase. These staircases are deliberately made into ornamental elements, like large-scale technological sculptures.[12]

The staircase in each lobby is a unique expression of this ideal. The Service administration lobby has a spinal-beam steel structure supporting travertine treads in metal pans; the Research administration lobby has a spiral staircase that floats granite treads supported by a converging double cone of stainless steel tension rods, much like the spokes on a bicycle wheel; and the Styling administration's staircase supports white terrazzo treads with thin, vertical stainless steel suspension rods that float above a reflecting pool. All of these stairs required technically challenging solutions and were achieved thanks to close collaboration among the architect, consultant engineers, and construction contractors.

left

Page from *General Motors Engineering Journal*, with illustrations showing the Research administration building's spiral staircase, May–June 1956

right

Spiral staircase in the Research administration building lobby, ca. 1955

Fountain mechanism for Alexander
Calder's *Water Ballet*, July 25, 1955

The landscape plan was developed by the Saarinen office and Thomas Dolliver Church.[13] Olav Hammarstrom from the Saarinen office rendered detailed planting illustrations—evidence that the Saarinen office was the lead on this part of the project. Edward Eichstedt provided on-site supervision and fulfillment services. The site plan is one of understated simplicity with a controlled rhythm, in concert with the buildings and open spaces. In Eichstedt's words:

> Streets are lined with shade trees, some in double rows, some single; and in some instances where it is desired to direct the interest toward the buildings, street trees have been omitted. The plantings are arranged to suggest direction and movement, and to complement the lines and masses of the buildings....The plan includes no axial construction, no monumental allées. The spaces are designed to flow into each other without ostentation.[14]

During the construction phase, Eichstedt managed the planting of more than 155 acres of lawn, 3,180 shrubs, 55,941 ground cover plants, and 13,000 trees, which were placed to line the roads and walkways, screen parking areas, provide shade to the buildings, and provide a buffer of forest at the perimeter of the campus.[15]

There are three bodies of water on the original Saarinen campus, constructed with shallow banks of river stone and concrete curbs. The twenty-two-acre central lake features islands planted with weeping willow trees and two large fountains. On the west side, a gigantic fountain forms a wall of water 115 feet long and 50 feet high, placed perpendicular to the main entrance. At the northwest corner of the lake, outside the Research lobby, is the *Water Ballet* fountain by Alexander Calder. The other two bodies of water are reflecting pools near Engineering and Styling, the latter of which has a small fountain. Additional landscape features include mushroom-shaped lighting fixtures that provide downcast light, pedestrian walkways, and parking lots.

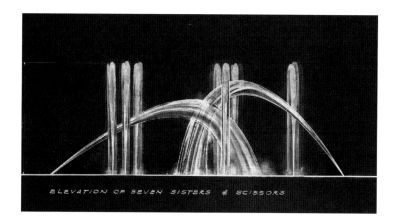

ELEVATION OF SEVEN SISTERS & SCISSORS

ELEVATION OF PLOPS

GENERAL MOTORS TECHNICAL CENTER

top left and right
Details of Saarinen, Saarinen and Associates' architectural drawing of the action and elevation of Alexander Calder's *Water Ballet*, ca. 1950

bottom left
Installation of the Hauserman system panels in the Engineering Dynamometer building, February 8, 1951

bottom right
Columnless construction of the Styling studio building, April 1, 1955

One of the overall goals for the campus was to provide flexibility in space planning for future modification. For instance, the office buildings were designed with no interior columns, and movable partition systems were developed to define spaces. All modernist designers were exploring modular elements at that time but had rarely put them into practice; the GM Technical Center project provided an opportunity to tie this concept to the automobile industry as a metaphor, applying the assembly-line approach to building construction techniques. Saarinen commented:

General Motors is a metal-working industry; it is a precision industry; it is a mass-production industry. All these things should, in a sense, be expressed in the architecture of its Technical Center. Thus, the design is based on steel—the metal of the automobile. Like the automobile itself, the buildings are essentially put together, as on an assembly line, out of mass-produced units. And, down to the smallest detail, we tried to give the architecture the precise, well-made look which is a proud characteristic of industrial America. The architecture attempts to find its eloquence out of a consistent and logical development of its industrial character.[16]

top left
Ceiling installation, second floor of the Engineering administration building, August 29, 1950

top right
Inspecting a plastic illumination panel, April 9, 1951

bottom
Lighting installation in the Styling administration building, February 17, 1955

The systems approach, inherent in the campus design, led to the development of interchangeable building components. These were standardized on a uniform five-foot module that repeats itself throughout the exterior and interior construction. Committing to this modular structure, Saarinen gave every building a character of its own, with slight differences in the expression of the rectangular grid: "Our basic design allowed variety within unity. The standardization of module throughout the project was arrived at for practical reasons, but we also hoped the constant use of this one dimension would have a unifying effect."[17] This practice reflects his father's idea to always design to the next-larger context; these building components facilitated a rhythmic interplay that radiated throughout the project.

The interior ceiling grid system also reinforced this unification. The Saarinen office worked with the Wakefield Brass Company in Vermilion, Ohio, on designing integrated modules to house speakers and fire-suppression apparatus as well as plastic illumination panels for diffuse lighting, which also conceal plumbing, electrical, and other mechanical systems (heating, high-velocity ventilation, air-conditioning). This integrated system was considered a highly significant advancement in building economy and comfort. GM worked directly with outside companies such as Caldwell and Thermotank to develop new technologies that would go on to be used in many building applications because the end results were so efficient and cost effective.[18] Warren Platner designed the vertical baffles into a V section of perforated steel and evaluated his designs with full-size mock-ups.[19]

The five-foot module was employed to delineate interiors, too. A prefabricated thin-walled system, manufactured by E. F. Hauserman with integrated doors, walls, and glazing panels, could be rearranged as functional or staffing requirements evolved. As noted by George Moon:

> The first Hauserman panels were delivered for the Engineering Building in March 1950. The panels were unique in their slimness, their flush, elegant detailing, and their clean, new color of beige, rather than the normal gray or green. Many things were special for the Technical Center. The height, which varied by area functions, was not the normal 8 or 9 feet, but 10 or more. Due to the five-foot module, rather than four, it became necessary to reduce the weight of the panels, so that they could be moved more easily. Saarinen, along with GM, convinced the steel mills to not only run 60″ wide steel sheet rolls, but to use a lighter gauge, less weighted steel. The panels, fabricated in the Cleveland plant, were loaded into boxcars, from the ends toward the middle, with the accessory pieces in the mid-section; care in transport was extremely important. In the completed walls, GM opted to use both steel and wood doors. While Hauserman made the steel doors, Eggers Company made the wood doors, and Sargeant made the very unique hardware....The Hauserman partitions and wall systems were used in every building on the Technical Center site.[20]

left
Hauserman partitions in offices at Service section administration building, May 24, 1955

right
Close-up of vertical lighting baffles, January 11, 2006

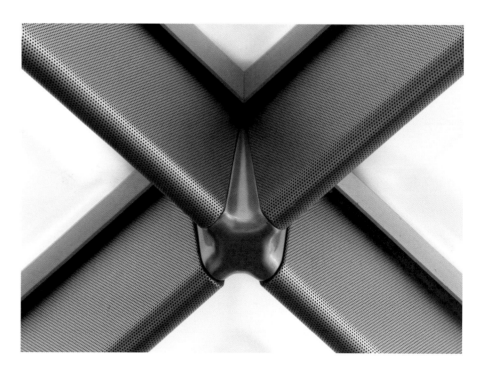

The building facades utilize a curtain wall system comprising steel, glass, and insulated wall panels at top and bottom, framed with aluminum. The panels have varying dimensional differences in the overall rectangular grid that defines each building's exterior. Although panel systems were being explored at the time, they had not yet been developed or used widely in architectural applications. The Saarinen firm designed a prefabricated solution with a two-inch-thick sandwich of honeycomb kraft paper, faced on both sides by either #20-gauge or #18-gauge steel sheets that were porcelain-enameled and filled with an insulating, noncombustible, granular material, like perlite.[21] This honeycomb-core design traced back to wartime research to develop a rigid, weatherproof material for military aircraft applications as well as porcelain enameling on thinner steel. Saarinen integrated this new technology in the development of the panels for the Technical Center. The panels required extensive modification throughout the testing process, which was directed primarily by Joseph Lacy, who recalled:

> I couldn't locate a manufacturer that would make a panel of our design. After a long search, I finally discovered that during the war the Chrysler Automobile Company made a prefabricated panel for the Army to be used in buildings in Alaska. The panel design was just what we wanted. They consisted of aluminum skins bonded to a core of insulating material. General Motors would not agree to the baked enamel finish so I proposed substituting [a] porcelain enamel finish instead of baked enamel. That was easier said than done as no one made such a panel. Chrysler was not interested in the job. Finally, I located a firm in Massachusetts that did porcelain enameling and they got the job for the first building. We had problems with the first panels. The metal used was sheet steel, as porcelain enamel could not be applied to aluminum. In firing the panel the heat warped the steel and it was almost impossible to flatten it out when it was bonded to the core material. Also, we had problems with the bond between the steel. We finally managed to get reasonably good results. Later on, another firm became interested in making panels and they gave us a better price and did a better job.[22]

The double-glazed windows were constructed with reflective, heat-absorbing glass with a slight blue-green tint. Kevin Roche recalled:

> John Dinkeloo was wonderful because I'd give him an idea and he'd go with it and really work it out. I had seen a photograph, the cover of a *Look* magazine, which had a person with sunglasses. So, I said to John, Why can't we do reflecting glass? He took it and he ran with it. The three of us: John, Eero, and I, went down to Toledo, where there were two or three glass manufacturing centers, and they laughed at us, at the idea that you could do a reflecting glass. But then John found somebody to do it, and that was the first building [in] which we were able to use reflecting glass.[23]

The Styling building was the only one not built with heat-absorbing reflective glass because of the possibility that the tint could skew color evaluation.[24]

Leakage was a major issue with the panels and with the window seals as well. Ultimately, a solution was achieved through experimentation in a collaboration among the architect, the contractor, the GM Inland Manufacturing division, and an entity referred to as "Field Supervision" in GM records. They first tried to adapt the rubber gaskets used in automotive

windshield applications, but rubber did not perform well, as it was easily damaged during the window installation process. Caulk also failed as an effective sealant because it allowed water to leak into the interiors.[25] A specially designed die-formed neoprene ultimately provided a successful seal. According to George Moon, GM patented it under the trademarked name Inilock, but it did not prove to be a profitable operation, and they ultimately sold the patent.[26]

The brightly colored glazed bricks used on both interior and exterior walls were another technical innovation that became an iconic design element of the campus. Their development was an extraordinary collaborative effort between the architect, manufacturers, and ceramic specialists. Lacy led this process:

> The only glazed bricks available at that time were pastel shades on perfectly smooth surfaces with no texture. The Saarinens wanted bright colors on bricks having an interesting textured surface. I exhausted the source of brick manufacturers without turning one up that made the kind of bricks we wanted. Finally, I obtained several unglazed bricks with a nice surface texture and then had the ceramicist at Cranbrook [Maija Grotell] apply a bright red glaze and fire them in her small kiln. They turned out to be just what we wanted, so I showed them to the agent for the bricks and he took the samples to the manufacturer. They said it would require a special kiln to do what we wanted, and it was finally agreed that General Motors would finance a special kiln for them if they agreed not to sell any similar bricks to the general trade.
>
> I consulted with a man at the General Motors spark plug division in Flint who was an expert in ceramics. From him I learned how to specify the glazing process in order to obtain a permanent glaze. One essential requirement was that the bricks had to have a certain factor of moisture absorption. If bricks below the minimum were used, the bricks would absorb too much water, which might freeze and pop the glaze off the surface.
>
> There were about sixteen different colors used on the buildings, and all were OK except one. In order to produce the color selected for the Power Plant, the manufacturer used bricks that were too soft. After the exterior of the building was finished a storm developed with a driving rain…and in the afternoon the temperature dropped below freezing, causing a disaster. The glaze popped off very badly. The bricks had to be removed and replaced with a slightly different color that could be applied to bricks hard enough to be above the minimum absorption limit.[27]

The common brick was Wyandot Sand Mold, 2¼ by 3¾ by 8 inches, specially burned in kilns at Claycraft Company in Upper Sandusky, Ohio, and then shipped to their Columbus, Ohio, plant, where it was burned for a second time with the specially developed glaze applied on the face.[28] This brick, because of the glaze, cost roughly three times the price of the unglazed unit.[29] Maija Grotell, the ceramicist at Cranbrook, participated in the development of the glazes, but the colors were specified by Alexander Girard, a consultant to the Saarinen firm, and Claycraft matched those colors.[30] Eleven intense colors were developed: deep crimson, scarlet, tangerine orange, lemon yellow, chartreuse, royal blue, sky blue, tobacco gray, brown, black, and white. These bricks were used for both exterior and interior applications, but a standard commercial flat-gray face was used most often in stairways and corridors, executive suites, and meeting rooms.[31] The interior bricks were modular series 2⅔ by 8 inches.[32]

top
Installing a neoprene gasket,
ca. 1952

bottom
Early glazed-brick experiments,
ca. 1950

top
Close-up of glazed brick in royal blue,
July 25, 2014

bottom left
Removing the glazed brick from the
powerhouse, November 11, 1950

bottom right
Standard commercial flat-gray face
brick commonly used in Technical
Center stairways, corridors, executive
suites, and meeting rooms, 2018

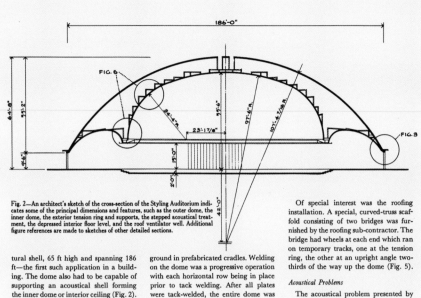

Fig. 2—An architect's sketch of the cross-section of the Styling Auditorium indicates some of the principal dimensions and features, such as the outer dome, the inner dome, the exterior tension ring and supports, the stepped acoustical treatment, the depressed interior floor level, and the roof ventilator well. Additional figure references are made to sketches of other detailed sections.

tural shell, 65 ft high and spanning 186 ft—the first such application in a building. The dome also had to be capable of supporting an acoustical shell forming the inner dome or interior ceiling (Fig. 2).

The outer dome was designed to be supported on a circumferential channel tension ring, 9 ft 6 in. above the ground level, supported on columns. The circumferential channel tension ring (Fig. 3) had a structural function as well as being an architectural design detail.

The erection of the dome was a predetermined, step-by-step procedure. After completing the reinforced concrete sub-structure and first floor slab, a central tower of scaffolding was erected, supplemented by gin-poles, jib-booms, and shores to facilitate the placing of the pie-shaped, two-way curved plates. Next, exterior columns and the exposed facia tension ring were erected. Initially the ring was tack-welded, then continuously welded when the circle was complete.

A top roof-ventilator well was then placed on top of the scaffold tower, and the top horizontal row of plates was erected (Fig. 4). Following this step, plates were erected from the tension ring up, in the plane of the horizontal curve. After several sections were in place, it was possible to put up double plate sections, and later it was possible to put up triple plate sections thereby reducing the time and cost of welding. These pre-formed plates were welded together on the

ground in prefabricated cradles. Welding on the dome was a progressive operation with each horizontal row being in place prior to tack welding. After all plates were tack-welded, the entire dome was continuously welded.

Of special interest was the roofing installation. A special, curved-truss scaffold consisting of two bridges was furnished by the roofing sub-contractor. The bridge had wheels at each end which ran on temporary tracks, one at the tension ring, the other at an upright angle two-thirds of the way up the dome (Fig. 5).

Acoustical Problems

The acoustical problem presented by the circular plan and curved ceiling of

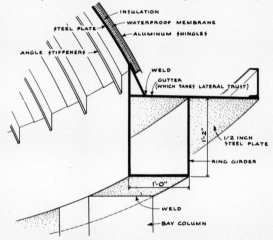

Fig. 3—An architect's sketch illustrates the detail of the Auditorium facia tension ring at the circumference of the outer dome. As is typical with many of the Technical Center buildings, the structural steel has continuously welded connections, and, as shown here, the steel remains exposed as a design feature. The ⅜-in. steel plate dome is weather tight; however, it is covered with weathering aluminum shingles and insulation for economy in heating and air conditioning.

Perhaps the most iconic building on the campus is the aluminum-clad Styling auditorium. Kevin Roche came up with the initial idea for this dome-shaped structure, based on the construction of a water tank. John Dinkeloo took on the challenge with SH&G and engineered a completely unique self-supporting structure, 65 feet high and 186 feet in diameter, which was built by the Chicago Bridge & Iron Company. The outer structural dome is made from welded ⅜-inch steel plates, which are supported by a steel channel attached to a tension ring, ultimately covered with insulation and a waterproof membrane and finished with nine-by-five-foot aluminum shingles. George Moon recalled the construction details:

A special scaffolding was developed to facilitate the aluminum installation, a structure that was curved to the dome's contour, and traveled around on wheels that fit into the tension ring gutter at the bottom, and rolled along the surface of the dome at the top. The pre-curved, pie-shaped pieces were placed with an overlap, and screwed in place, on an average 12 screws to a panel.[33]

Illustrations of the Styling auditorium in *General Motors Engineering Journal*, May–June 1956

Construction of the Styling
auditorium's domed roof; from top
left: January 7, February 4, August 15,
and late 1955

overleaf
Styling patio and auditorium as seen
from the roof of the studio building,
December 12, 1955

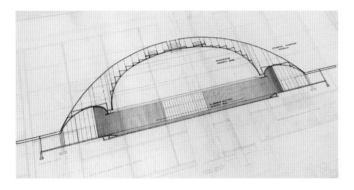

The inner sky dome is made of ⅛-inch perforated steel suspended by rods from the outer shell.[34] The curved white ceiling was designed to mimic an overcast sky condition, ideal for evaluating the complex, highly reflective surfaces of a vehicle.[35] Lights are installed around the dome's base to illuminate the ceiling indirectly, much like sunlight cast from below the horizon. (Architectural models were built incorporating this indirect interior lighting to test its effect on model cars.) To achieve a smooth ceiling surface, the architects and engineers devised compound-curved, trapezoidal panels that attached over pads, solving the acoustical and aesthetic issues. This sandwiched structure has remarkable structural integrity and is thinner than an eggshell when compared in scale.

Another iconic feature is the water tower. Construction of this structure was delayed until the end of 1953 due to shortages of steel during the Korean War. By then the lake was in place and had to be drained to build the water tower. The same company that built the Styling auditorium was chosen to build the 250,000-gallon elevated tank.

GENERAL MOTORS TECHNICAL CENTER
WARREN TOWNSHIP—MACOMB COUNTY—MICH.

Subject: Site Development: Elevated Water Tower
Showing Operation By: GMEC
View From: N-175.0'   E-330.0'
Torrent: Northwest
G. M. Photo Section   Date: 7-7-54   Neg. 91248 - 1

TITLE: Wind Tunnel. Car Entrance is at Left.   VIEW TOWARD: SE   DATE: 9-23-53   NEG.# X2308-583
       Roof is Being Finished.   FROM: Construction Shanty
                                                                          Roof.

TITLE: Turbine Test Bldg.   Small Cell Exhaust   VIEW TOWARD: South   DATE: 7/18/52   NEG.# X2308-186
       Cubicles   FROM: Turbine Bldg. Roof

Major structures at the Technical Center were completed by 1955, with the construction of minor buildings and site work continuing into 1956. During this time, several additional building projects were added and carried out. For instance, a decision was made while the foundation work was underway to add an underground tunnel system for pedestrian travel among all of the buildings. In 1951 a one-mile-long "check road" (a test track) was added to allow the Engineering staff to conduct vehicle tests on-site.[36] In 1952 the Wind Tunnel Building was added for the study of air velocity, temperature, and direction on the operation of vehicles, as was the Gas Turbine Laboratory, built to provide functional test facilities for a variety of gas turbine engines that General Motors was developing for automotive applications.[37] In 1953 the Isotope Research Laboratory was added for the peacetime use of atomic by-products in engineering and research.[38]

The very influential but largely unacknowledged collaborators in this project were the many job shops and suppliers in the Detroit area that supported the automobile industry. The Saarinen firm used these resources to their full advantage, as Roche described:

> You cannot overstress the importance of Detroit in the postwar period…including the music….I don't know if they're really aware how important they were at that moment in time.…You can get anything made there. It was amazing. There were tiny little workshops, privately owned. You could just go and make a series of whatever—chairs or ladders or stoves or whatever. You could get almost anything made. I remember working with a hardware store of some sort to try and get the lever and handle and the lock and all that organized in a simple modern way. You couldn't just go to someplace and buy anything. It didn't exist, except for the Victorian decoration.[39]

The construction of the original General Motors Technical Center campus spanned 1949 to 1956. The division of work in dollar volume was approximately 20 percent to the Saarinen firm and 80 percent to SH&G.

left
Construction on the Wind Tunnel building, September 23, 1953

right
Construction on the Gas Turbine Laboratory, July 18, 1952

GENERAL MOTORS CORPORATION
GENERAL MOTORS BUILDING
DETROIT

September 14, 1955

Dear Member of Styling:

It is indeed a pleasure to welcome you to our new
building. General Motors Styling has the finest
talent and craftsmen in the industry and now the
finest facilities.

With the privilege of working in this handsome
building goes the responsibility of each one of us
for keeping it in the best possible condition. As
we enjoy the many conveniences and the beauty of
our new quarters, we must maintain it as we would
our own homes.

Styling continues to have an important and challenging job to do for General Motors. May our future
here be as pleasant as the past years have been.
Welcome to the Technical Center.

Very truly yours,

Harley J. Earl

mjo

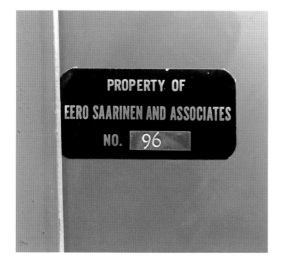

left
Label from Eero Saarinen and
Associates office files

right
Welcome letter from Styling Vice
President Harley Earl to his staff,
September 14, 1955

Eliel Saarinen died on July 1, 1950:

It was quite sudden. One evening after Eliel and his wife, Loja, had finished
dinner, Loja and Eliel had gone to their favorite chairs. After a bit Loja reminded
him that it was time for their favorite radio program. He didn't respond and
she went to see what the delay was and found that he had suddenly died of
a heart attack.[40]

The name of the firm was changed to Eero Saarinen and Associates.
The partners from the previous firm—Eero, Joseph Lacy, and J. Henderson
Barr—remained.[41] Construction work on the Technical Center was largely
complete by September 1955, when staff in the last building group, Styling,
began to move in and set up operations. This unofficially marked the completion
of the construction phase of the Technical Center.[42] But one important event
had yet to occur: a dedication to introduce the campus to the world.

CHAPTER FIVE

Dedication

opposite
The grandstand positioned along
the western edge of the lake at the
GM Technical Center dedication,
May 15, 1956

above
Audience members (top) viewing the
Futurama diorama (bottom), built for
the 1939 World's Fair in New York on
behalf of General Motors by Norman
Bel Geddes, 1939

Twelve years had passed since the first discussion between Alfred Sloan and Charles Kettering about the idea of relocating GM's technical staffs to a campus in suburban Detroit. More than eight years had passed since the project had been embraced, designed, excavated, halted, abandoned, and resurrected, during which time the architectural lead role passed from father, Eliel Saarinen, to son, Eero Saarinen. The cost had initially been estimated at $20 million, then revised to $25 to $30 million (mentioned by Eero in the letter reproduced on page 59), before eventually ballooning to $150 million by the time of its completion.[1]

The United States had itself changed dramatically during this period, with unprecedented economic growth that was in many respects a direct result of the automobile and its effect on the nation's expanding suburbs, where more than twice the number of cars were registered in 1956 than in 1945.[2] There was pent-up demand for products that embodied the transformative lifestyle made possible by postwar prosperity. The year 1956 heralded record employment and personal income and topped the seven-year run of the second-largest bull market in US stock history. During that period, the Dow-Jones Industrial Average jumped more than 300 percent, from 160 to 524 points.[3] GM promoted the creation of a national highway system through its "Better Highways" essay contest.[4] Construction of the interstate highway system was authorized by the Federal Aid Highway Act of 1956, which further cemented the automobile as the embodiment of mobility, individuality, and freedom.[5]

GM was at the forefront of designing this new postwar American aesthetic with its iconic and dramatic automotive styling and its bright and cheery new Frigidaire appliances. GM built cars for every buyer and created an aspirational culture through its tiered brands and the anticipation of the new annual models. Early on GM had promoted this culture of the suburban future by sponsoring such events as the City of Tomorrow presentation at the 1939 World's Fair, which attracted more than five million visitors and was voted the fair's most popular exhibit in a Gallup poll.[6] Industrial designer Norman Bel Geddes had created that exhibit, and by coincidence, Eero Saarinen had worked briefly at his New York office as a draftsman for the Futurama portion.[7] This dramatic experience took the visitor through a twenty-minute "carry-go-round" over and through a huge scale model of the City of Tomorrow, an imagined vision of the suburban landscape of 1960:

> Come tour the future with General Motors! A transcontinental flight over America in 1960. What will we see? What changes will transpire? This magic Aladdin-like flight through time and space is Norman Bel Geddes's conception of the many wonders that may develop in the not-too-distant future....This world of tomorrow is a world of beauty.[8]

top
GM Streamliner buses lined
up in front of the General Motors
Building in Detroit, Michigan,
January 29, 1936

center
Crowds gather at the Parade
of Progress exhibitions and
the GM Futurliner concept bus,
September 16, 1955

bottom
A 1956 GMC Fleetside Pickup
displays a Frigidaire product to be
awarded to the seven millionth
visitor to the GM Parade of Progress
at the National Orange Show
Grounds, San Bernardino, California,
March 2, 1956

This utopian notion of the future underpinned GM promotional events such as the 1941 Parade of Progress and its hugely popular Motorama shows— elaborate, stunning traveling exhibitions that showcased some of GM's most innovative and revolutionary dream cars. These shows captured the imagination of the public and set the stage for the new Technical Center as the embodiment of the corporate suburban ideal.

The Saarinen office began the Technical Center project with about ten employees and by the late 1950s had grown to 110.[9] Eero leveraged the notoriety of this large commission that had expanded his firm. He embraced the publicity opportunity by crafting a thoughtful and effective public relations strategy to communicate his overall design philosophy, which resonated with the national postwar culture. He promoted the idea that his clients and their culture were his "cocreators" in service to society and offered the media conceptual and visual evidence that illustrated this ideal with profound elegance. Every form of communication (television, radio, newspapers, magazines, exhibitions, professional journals, advertisements) that existed in the United States in the 1950s covered the Technical Center project from its inception to its completion, reaching far beyond the typical architecture audience.[10] The General Motors public relations juggernaut also helped create and satisfy an international thirst for information about their new "Technopolis."[11] Many new commissions for the Saarinen firm resulted, including several that came about during the construction of the Technical Center: facilities for John Deere, International Business Machines (IBM), and the Columbia Broadcasting System (CBS); a chapel for the Massachusetts Institute of Technology (MIT); the Miller House in Columbus, Indiana; and terminals for Trans World Airlines (TWA) at John F. Kennedy International Airport (then known as Idlewild) in New York and Dulles International Airport in Washington, DC.

Overhead view of the GM Motorama display at the Waldorf Astoria hotel in New York, January 18, 1953

RADIO AND TV

MAGAZINE

SPECIAL SECTIONS

SPECIAL

SPECIAL SECTIONS

SPECIAL SECTIONS

BEDFORD DAILY TIMES

WASHINGTON NEWS
7 PAGES

TOLEDO BLADE
12 PAGES

SAN FRANCISCO CHRONICLE

PONTIAC

HORSEPOWER

SPECIAL SECTIONS

IT WAS NEWS

when General Motors dedicated
its Technical Center and whetted
America's interest in the future.

THIS DISPLAY PROVIDES ONE MEASURE OF THAT INTEREST.

It includes a representative sampling
of newspaper, magazine, radio and television coverage of the dedication.

Shown here are:

1. Some of the 78 newspaper special sections devoted
   to the Technical Center.

2. News Stories by reporters who covered the event.

3. Magazine articles.

4. Reports on radio and television coverage.

DEPARTMENT OF PUBLIC RELATIONS

At this new Technical Center we

Probing for Engine Progress: General Motors Research men keep seeking to make today's piston engines more efficient. Here, a high-speed camera peers through a quartz window cut into an experimental one-cylinder engine—increases knowledge of combustion.

Pioneering the Way in Power: The problem of perfecting the automotive gas turbine engine requires a deep knowledge of thermodynamics, painstaking design, new metallurgy, skilled craftsmanship, and the most advanced testing facilities. Above, GM Research men are hard at work on the highly promising Whirlfire GT-304 gas turbine engine, used in the experimental laboratory-on-wheels—Firebird II.

Sculpting the Shape of the Future: Over a thousand stylists and technicians at the vast new Technical Center are working to shape the future in automotive and other product design. Above, the rear section of the Firebird II is being sculptured in plaster during preliminary design stages.

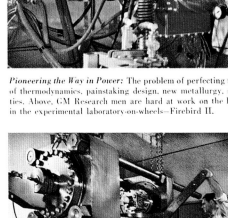

Testing Metals for Tomorrow: This huge fatigue-testing machine tests metals for ability to stand up under punishment. The new Technical Center has one of the world's most elaborate experimental foundries, where metallurgists produce better metals for the world of tomorrow.

New Horizons in Health: In laboratories like this, GM scientists engage in many projects seldom identified with industrial arts. These include such humanitarian developments as the first mechanical heart and the Centri-Filmer for purifying vaccines.

This advertisement will a

Saturday Evening Post, May 19, 1956   Look, Ju
Life, May 28, 1956   Time, M
Collier's, June 8, 1956

Left to Right: Main Research Building, Service Building, Manufacturing Development Building (behind water tower), Engineering Building, Styling Building and Styling Auditorium Dome facing 22-acre lake, focal point of GM Technical Center.

welcome the challenge of the future

WE HAVE JUST dedicated one of the most far-reaching industrial projects ever undertaken by an American business.

It is the vast General Motors Technical Center, built on 330 acres of beautifully landscaped campus northeast of Detroit.

More than four thousand scientists, engineers, stylists and technicians are at work within its twenty-five modern air-conditioned buildings—making it the largest institution in the world devoted to progress in the industrial arts and sciences.

As such, through Research, Engineering and Styling it helps make next year's automobiles, home appliances, Diesel engines and our other products better than this year's models.

Beyond that, at the Technical Center men of inquiring minds are delving into the unknown in search of new materials, new forces, new techniques that will maintain America's technological leadership for generations to come.

Here scientists are rearranging molecules and repatterning alloys to produce sturdier metals, more efficient lubricants, more powerful fuels.

Here engineers are experimenting with ways and means of adapting these discoveries to the production of more useful things for the public.

Here stylists are plotting new designs that will insure greater beauty, comfort and convenience in the shape of things to come.

One result of all this—seen by millions at our recent Motoramas—is GM's latest dream car Firebird II. Built of gleaming titanium, powered by a gas turbine engine and styled like a jet aircraft, it may foreshadow the motorcar of tomorrow.

But the horizons of the Technical Center stretch far beyond the motor vehicle into many diverse and fruitful activities for the common good. It has already developed the first successful mechanical heart, a new Centri-Filmer for purifying vaccines, and is engaged in many important humanitarian projects.

Thus equipped, General Motors welcomes the challenge of the future. We hope to open new fields of knowledge that will help to build an even more dynamic and prosperous national economy —and attract more and more young people to technical careers.

in technical progress
GENERAL MOTORS
leads the way

See the GM Technical Center on TV—NBC—Sunday afternoon, May 20.

e following publications:

Newsweek, May 21, 1956
U.S. News & World Report, May 25, 1956
Fortune, June, 1956

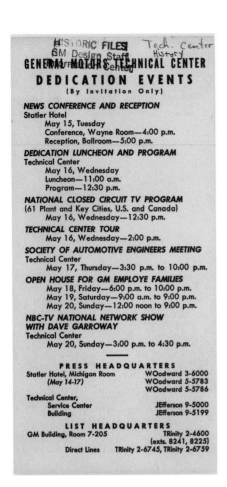

For General Motors, the completion of the campus represented the realization of the great dream first envisioned by Sloan and Kettering in 1944: to gather all GM's product development activities in one central location in state-of-the-art facilities that would enable the corporation to be *the* world leader in technological progress, from research to engineering to design. GM's public relations staff churned out voluminous materials to support the story of the campus and its function. Advertisements were placed in the country's major newspapers and magazines—*Fortune*, *Time*, *Newsweek*—declaring, "We welcome the challenge of the future at this new Technical Center."[12] Some of the ads featuring current GM vehicles were staged on the campus, such as one portraying a woman driving her new Pontiac Catalina with the caption "Here's where new ideas come from...and here's where they GO!"[13] GM also featured the Technical Center in many of its own publications, such as the *General Motors Engineering Journal*, which was directed at scientists and engineers, and *GM Folks*, an internal publication for all employees.[14]

GM planned an extraordinary series of events to introduce the campus to the world and formally mark the beginning of this new era. It was a full-on media extravaganza in which GM associated itself with the prosperity of the nation. Three days before the official dedication, the *New York Times Magazine* announced, "With atomic energy, jet engines, automation and other scientific revolutions erasing the boundary between university and factory, scientists are becoming as fundamental as salesmen in industry's scheme of things."[15]

On Monday, May 14, 1956, one day before the dedication, GM sponsored a national radio program featuring such media impresarios as broadcaster Edward R. Murrow; commentators Gabriel Heatter and Hans von Kaltenborn; and economist, author, and journalist Henry J. Taylor, who declared, "General Motors welcomes the challenge of the future. General Motors hopes to open new fields of knowledge that will help to build an even more dynamic and prosperous national economy—and to keep America strong, mighty America, your land and mine. Good night. God bless our country."[16]

The formal dedication ceremony on May 15 and 16, 1956, was attended by an audience of more than five thousand of the nation's science, engineering, education, and industrial leaders and was covered by 250 members of the press.[17] The master of ceremonies was national television anchor Walter Cronkite, who introduced the lead speakers: Harlow H. Curtice, General Motors president; Dr. Lawrence R. Hafstad, vice president of Research; and Charles F. Kettering, director and research consultant. A special feature of the program was a closed-circuit telecast from the White House by President Dwight D. Eisenhower. These men spoke of creating an environment that would enable resident GM staff to solve problems, hasten the pace of technological progress, and transform the future. Curtice remarked:

> We expect to continue our contributions to technological progress—and at an accelerated rate....The buildings are furnished with every conceivable type of tool, equipment, testing device—all the latest and the very best. Working conditions, likewise, are the very best. The campus-like atmosphere was sought deliberately, not to impress visitors, but because we believe that such surroundings stimulate creative thinking and are conducive to good work.[18]

Hafstad was a well-respected scientist in the field of atomic energy who in 1939 had created the first nuclear fission reaction in the United States. He served as executive secretary of the Research and Development board

at the US Department of Defense and was the first director of the Reactor Development division of the US Atomic Energy Commission before joining GM as vice president of Research in September 1955. The title of his speech at the dedication was "The Future Is Our Assignment":

> These are exciting times in which to live....With wisdom brought to bear upon all the problems of our society, this second industrial revolution will not stop until the standard of living of the entire world has been raised to undreamed of heights. This, then, is the meaning of this great Technical Center: a symbol of faith in the future and of confidence in our social system; an instrument and a tool for increased production and an ever higher standard of living—an insurance policy against ignorance and fear of the unknown and unexpected, a center of knowledge, a home for the inquiring mind—this is the General Motors Technical Center. May we live up to our opportunities.[19]

Kettering, Hafstad's predecessor as head of Research, had been instrumental in the initial concept of the Technical Center. He spoke to the crowd next, describing the facility as "a great intellectual golf course where we can go out and practice.... Here in this institution we have a place where we can make indefinite practice shots, and the only time we don't want to fail is the last time we try it."[20]

top
An audience watches a closed-circuit address from President Dwight D. Eisenhower in the Styling auditorium at the dedication, May 15, 1956

bottom
Charles Kettering addresses the crowd at the dedication, May 15, 1956

And finally, Eisenhower summed up his thoughts:

This particular Center is a place for leadership in furthering new attacks on the
technological frontier. Beyond that frontier lie better and fuller employment,
opportunities for people to demonstrate yet again the value of a system based
on the dignity of the human being, and on their free opportunities in life. Beyond
it lie people, better capable of working with others and so that they may share
what they learn with our friends in the world.[21]

Notably, there was no mention of the architect. When asked about this
omission, Kevin Roche described his experience sitting in the back during the
ceremony with Aline Bernstein (Louchheim) Saarinen (Eero's wife) and
John Dinkeloo:

Aline got upset about that because she had a strong PR touch, and I don't think
I'm being inaccurate in saying that he [Eero] was pretty much passed over in
the whole thing. But then I can understand that because they [GM] all invested
so much of themselves into it.[22]

The program was carried on a closed-circuit telecast to sixty-one cities
across the United States and Canada, where more than fifteen thousand
GM officials and civic, military, education, and industrial leaders had gathered
for dedication luncheons.[23] Simultaneously, GM plants throughout the country

1956 GM XP-500 experimental
vehicle on display west of the lake,
early 1960s

staged open-house programs, welcoming their employees' families and the
public to visit their facilities. There were guided tours, press conferences, and
receptions. On May 20 a special edition of the national NBC show *Wide Wide
World*, hosted by Dave Garroway, took place at the Technical Center. The special,
called "Promise to America," was a ninety-minute live television broadcast of the
popular variety show; it trumpeted: "This is the General Motors Technical Center,
a big place…big in dreams as well as size, big in its hope for the future and its
belief in its…PROMISE FOR AMERICA."[24] TV and radio personality Arthur
Godfrey, a good friend of Harley Earl's, drove a Firebird II gas-turbine car around
the site while a TV camera followed him.[25]

Campus tours featured displays demonstrating the activities of the
various disciplines. For instance, guests were introduced to a 137-foot-long
semiautomatic assembly machine that put together seventy-five parts of
a cylinder head mechanically; the first successful mechanical heart, a new
artificial lung, and other research firsts in medicine; a road test demonstration;
declassified military vehicle demonstrations; a flow table that showed a turbine
blade's effect on water flow patterns; styling studios dressed with the vehicles
and brand identity of each division; and the latest experimental automobile,
the XP-500.[26]

The PR department produced numerous publications, including two different
versions of a souvenir brochure titled *Where Today Meets Tomorrow*. The deluxe
version, complete with slipcase and introductory letter from Harlow H. Curtice,
was luxuriously produced, with a cover featuring a romantic night scene of the

top
Where Today Meets Tomorrow
booklet, 1956

bottom
Time magazine cover, July 2, 1956

108

campus in a heavily retouched photograph by Ezra Stoller. It was presented to attendees at the dedication and mailed to every employee who worked at the center. A smaller version had a cover beautifully illustrated with a George Sheppard painting of the Technical Center.[27] It was distributed to all visitors to the Technical Center open house during the weekend that followed the formal dedication ceremony. Both versions contained a carefully crafted text that explained the Technical Center's raison d'être and the types of activities that would take place there.

The reception by the popular and professional press was immediate, voluminous, and overwhelmingly positive. National and international writers from publications such as *House & Garden*, *Colliers*, *Women's Home Companion*, *Harper's*, *American*, *Vogue*, and *Popular Mechanics* covered the campus. *Life* magazine's declaration that "GM constructs a 'Versailles of Industry'" became perhaps the most-used catchphrase. *Life* sent its top staff photographer, Andreas Feininger, to document the project with six pages of large photographs illustrating its unusual beauty. *Time* magazine put Eero on the cover on July 2, 1956, with the site plan of the project in the background. *Fortune* magazine described a campus that

> conforms to the postwar fashion, but in its wedding of a great modern architect with G.M. engineering, it achieves a new serene integration....The achievement, which is Saarinen's, is to have held all this advanced technology under admirable control in designing an integrated series of buildings that are modern but not freakish, functional but not barren, imposing but not overblown, clean and cool in line but with an underlying warmth achieved through a bold orchestration and notable architectural use of color.[28]

Architectural Forum noted: "Just as the Acropolis was built to be contemplated by a man standing still, Venice to be enjoyed from a drifting gondola, GM Technical Center should best flash by a Buick window at 35 mph. The Technical Center site module is a speedometer."[29] The *Christian Science Monitor* described the project as an "Industrial Disneyland....Ask the man on the street corner [in Warren] the time of day, but don't be surprised if you get the answer: 'it is just about 5 to 10 years later than you think.'"[30] The *Detroit News* published a special pictorial magazine highlighting Dinah Shore, who was famous for hosting several Chevrolet-sponsored variety programs and singing the sponsor's theme song, "See the USA in Your Chevrolet." She was photographed in a dazzling red gown for the publication, which described the multimillion-dollar Technical Center as "probably the world's most beautiful workshop. Here, more than 4,700 persons are working to build a better tomorrow. It is a workshop, not only for researchers, stylists and designers, but for mechanics, machinists and engineers as well."[31] Numerous companies in the Detroit area took out ads congratulating GM on the opening of its campus, many using the iconic water tower in the background.

Less than two months after the dedication, an article in *Architectural Record* named the campus one of

> the fifty buildings and building groups nominated by a panel of fifty architects and scholars as the most significant in the past 100 years of architecture in America....Of the General Motors Technical Center, Architect Max Abramovitz writes: "The General Motors Group is one of the great 20th Century compositions born out of the sense of civic responsibility of a great corporation....Eero Saarinen's

grasp of his opportunity and his masterly solution in plan, form, color and detail rightly permit this group to be called the Industrial 'Versailles' of this period.... Rarely does a designer succeed in creating a structure that has a sense of belonging to the times, a sense of rhythm and counterpoint that is in tune with the personality of industry and the spirit of today."[32]

In the same article, little-known but influential modernist John Ekin Dinwiddie noted, "The General Motors Technical Center is the first and best complete collaboration of industry, architects and landscape architect."[33] And Morris Ketchum Jr. added:

top left and bottom right
GM Research employees, 1956

top right
Engineers studying gear fatigue, 1956

bottom left
Designers working in the studio at the Styling building, 1956

Here in a vast controlled environment created out of flat and empty farmland, precisely and beautifully interrelated buildings are served by appropriate routes for motor and pedestrian traffic, and lined to outdoor spaces for pools, gardens, parking and service areas. This huge project sums up all the current aims and current progress of American architecture—its technical achievements, its re-integration of all the building arts and its ability to handle both single buildings and building groups. As such, it is a milestone to be recognized and remembered.[34]

GENERAL MOTORS CORPORATION

GENERAL MOTORS BUILDING
DETROIT 2, MICHIGAN
TRINITY 2-4600

NEWS

FOR RELEASE IMMEDIATELY, MAY 21, 1956

DETROIT -- Almost one million visitors attended an international Open House at General Motors installations in the United States and Canada, celebrating dedication of the GM Technical Center, President Harlow H. Curtice announced today.

Doors were opened to the public at 114 GM plants, 15 Training Centers, and General Motors Institute at Flint, Mich. -- a total of 130 installations. In addition, the Technical Center at Warren, Mich., was open from Friday through Sunday to GM employees and their families.

Last of the Open Houses were held Sunday. Most were on Wednesday, when GM formally dedicated the research center where "today meets tomorrow."

The Technical Center itself drew 179,500 visitors at its Open House. Hundreds of thousands of other persons throughout the nation saw the center Sunday afternoon by means of a nationwide telecast, "A Promise for America," over the National Broadcasting Company Network.

Open House attendance in Detroit, including that at the Technical Center, totaled 226,230 -- plus 5,393 at nearby Livonia, 31,350 at Pontiac and 4,373 at Ypsilanti.

Elsewhere, attendance at the various Open Houses ranged up to 68,126 at the Buick plant at Flint. In that city, where attendance at 10 GM installations totaled 219,877, schools were closed Wednesday and busses provided free transportation to the plants.

At the Delco-Remy Division plant in Anderson, Ind., officials buried a "time capsule" to be opened 25 years from now. It contained pictures of 1956 GM experimental "dream cars" and messages from the presidents of Indiana universities.

"We in General Motors are extremely pleased that so many people visited us,"

(more)

Reportage on the opening of the Technical Center was filled with glowing praise and acceptance for this new type of intentional, collaborative architect-client relationship, which had created such dramatic and highly individualized technical and aesthetic solutions. Together, Eero Saarinen and his client General Motors had designed a new frontier of suburban corporate campus architecture that would influence the postwar US landscape for years to come in a profound and transformative way.

General Motors press release,
May 21, 1956

CHAPTER SIX

An Architecture of Interspaces

"Always design a thing by considering it in its next larger context—a chair in a room, a room in a house, a house in an environment, an environment in a city plan."
—Eliel Saarinen[1]

This profound expression of design intent by Eliel Saarinen was embraced by his son, Eero, and is reflected in the thoughtful interconnectedness of the General Motors Technical Center campus. The rectangular lake provides a grounding element that repeats itself in every direction, large and small. An internal and external hierarchy orders space in a decidedly nonhierarchical way, not subservient to any monument or defining structure. It has pulse— a rectangular rhythm that radiates and repeats from within. But even with its precise and refined construction, the organization is not static or slavish, as each building has its own defining resonance.

This expression of order and interconnectedness starts from the smallest interior detail. Detroit at the time was a nexus of modern design in the United States. Eero took advantage of that confluence by hiring a multitude of design consultants for the project. One of these was Ruth Adler Schnee. She and her husband and business partner, Edward Schnee, ran Adler-Schnee in Detroit's Harmonie Park, one of the first retail stores in the country to sell modern furniture, fabrics, and home furnishings. Adler Schnee recalled:

> In 1946 I had the great opportunity to have Eliel Saarinen as my instructor at Cranbrook. There, I learned of his meticulous attention to detail—also amply evident at the General Motors complex. Many years later, I was called to the GM Styling Building to work with Eero and his concept of a building as a total design: integrating not only the site and the structure, but also the furnishings, down to the design of eating utensils for use on the executives' dining table.[2]

Adler Schnee worked with Morris Jackson from the Saarinen office, who issued her this simple but ambitious design direction: "We want wonderful stuff!"[3]

For the executive dining room in the Styling building, the Schnees supplied white Rosenthal china with gold trim and Gordon Fraser stainless steel bowls, creamer pitchers, sugar containers, and salt and pepper shakers, as well as a Salton warming tray built into a credenza. Adler Schnee also designed an elaborate ceiling display made of different colors of Thaibok brand silk fabric attached around the ceiling perimeter and gathered at the center. Harley Earl, however, did not approve and had the entire room redesigned by in-house Styling designers.[4]

opposite
Technical Center offices, 1951

above
Place settings in the Styling building's executive dining room, known as the Blue Room, 1950s

113

Another of Eero's collaborators was textile designer Marianne Strengell, who viewed her materials as architectural elements, not adornments. In 1951 she was hired as a consultant to the Saarinen firm and worked closely with Warren Platner on design and color specifications for the lobbies and Central Restaurant. As explained in an article for *Handweaver & Craftsman* magazine, Strengell responded to Eero's desire

> to soften and humanize the great expanses of glass, the pre-fabricated units of walls, the use of stainless steel and aluminum with off-white terrazzo floors, and the desire of the client for strong, practical, masculine interiors. This meant careful planning of color for contrast as well as harmony, plus contrasts in texture.[5]

All of the rugs for the campus were designed by Strengell and handwoven by her longtime assistant, Gerda Nyberg. The rug for the lobby in the Research administration building measured an astounding eighteen by thirty-two feet and was handmade in pure wool. Surprisingly, these custom-made rugs and fabrics were not more expensive than commercially made rugs, because she worked directly with the mills.[6] However, when Harley Earl inquired how much the two large textural carpets for his Styling lobby cost and Strengell informed him that it was about $2,500 for the pair, he responded, "Good God, that's the price of a new Chevrolet!"[7]

Eero also collaborated with Florence Knoll on the interior furnishings. He designed chairs, tables, sofas, benches, and desks, which Knoll fabricated and manufactured. Placed throughout the campus, these Knoll-built pieces reaffirmed its visual language. The lobby of the Research administration building was furnished with a circular reception desk; beautiful Saarinen-designed tan leather seating with minimal chrome frames; a long, cushioned bench; and a unique marble table, all with the same leg detail. They were contemporary, stylish, functional, and beautifully crafted. George Moon recalled:

What Cranbrook did for American design is profound, and is no better exemplified than in the work done by Knoll, with Saarinen and with Eames. They learned the lessons well that were taught by Eliel, their mentor. He embued in them that sense of detail from the largest to the smallest item, and for the total relationship of all the arts and crafts that make up a complete composition. It was the Bauhaus humanized.[8]

left
Florence Knoll and Eero Saarinen
with Saarinen's Pedestal Chair, 1956

right
Chair for Harley Earl,
January 27, 1956

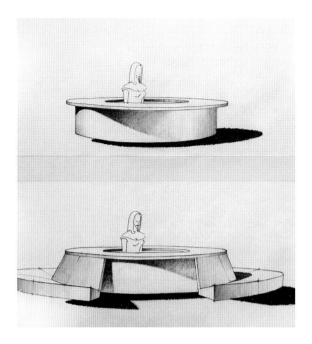

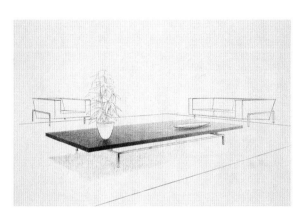

In addition to collaborating with outside consultants, the Saarinen firm also worked with GM Styling's Architecture and Interiors studio to design various spaces at the Technical Center. One of the more interesting aspects of their relationship was an agreement that specified which entity would be lead designer on certain interiors. The relationship with Engineering on its administration building was less formalized than that with Research, and Eero wanted to clarify the division of work for the remainder of the project. A March 26, 1951, letter from the Saarinen office noted:

We agreed that the best results would be obtained by a joint effort. In certain areas, Styling would take the lead and we would be merely consultants; in other areas, we would be the primary designers and Styling would act as consultants…. This seems to be an arrangement very satisfactory to both Styling and ourselves. We are interested in the lobbies because of the very intimate relationship between the architecture and the furnishings of these areas. The typical offices are fairly standard and therefore, it seems, can best be done jointly. This arrangement, of course, is subject to the wishes of the various tenants.[9]

top left
Renderings of reception desk in lobby of Research administration building, undated

bottom left
Rendering of low table in lobby of the Engineering administration building, undated

right
Agreement between GM and Eero Saarinen, signed November 14, 1952

Rendering of lobby design of the
Styling administration building by
Carl Benkert, early 1950s.

Review of design renderings and
material samples for the lobby of
the Styling administration building;
the "Damsels of Design" were a
group of women industrial designers
GM Styling hired in the 1950s. With
face visible, left to right: Jane Van
Alstyne, Helene Pollis, and Suzanne
Vanderbilt, March 12, 1956

Detail of laminated cherry furniture
in the office of Vice President of
Styling Harley Earl, undated

Bette Hardin, Harley Earl's secretary,
in his office, September 10, 1957

Styling was designated the primary designer of the executive offices and executive dining areas; the Saarinen office was the primary designer of lobbies, restaurants, and auditoriums; and the two worked jointly on typical offices and the libraries.[10]

The office of Vice President of Styling Harley Earl is a great example of this agreement—one of the most impressive and beautiful executive offices ever designed. Kevin Roche was the lead for the Saarinen firm and worked with John Dinkeloo as well as other consultants both inside and outside GM. The suite consists of two side-by-side rooms separated by a curved wall of fluted vertical lengths of cherrywood cased in aluminum trim. It is the only serpentine wall in the entire complex. In the office facing the lake, designated for Earl, there are two built-in seating areas, one of which leads into a floating, curvilinear desk made from laminated cherrywood. The desk is a visual metaphor for the old wooden Keller forms used in the vehicle evaluation process, over which hand-shaped sheet metal panels were formed. A chrome pedestal supports the cantilevered end. Warren Platner designed a thick plate-glass table that changes from coffee-table height to work height with the push of a button. Color consultant Alexander Girard specified the colors and fabric for the seating areas.[11]

Rendering of floating desk for
Harley Earl's office, undated

The redesign of the executive dining room at Styling, following Earl's rejection of the original Schnee decor, was directed by GM's head of Architecture and Interiors, Carl Benkert, and designer George Moon. This intimate twenty-foot-square space was worked out with an elaborate scale model that took eight weeks to develop before it was presented to Earl. According to Moon:

> The focal point of the room was the dining table. I developed a six-sided table, with two seating places at each face, or side. It was ten feet across, and was made of solid teak, two inches thick. The table was constructed in three large parts assembled on site. Due to the size and the difficulty in passing food items around, we developed a large "lazy susan," a rotating plate, 16 inches wide and six feet in diameter—made of ¼" aluminum plate, anodized in black, textured in a finely-scored, radiating, line pattern. At the push of a button (there was a button on the table edge between the two seats), the tray rotated in a clockwise direction powered by a television antenna rotation motor underneath. In the center of the table was a four-foot planter, filled with potted plants, and holding six, upward pointing floodlights.[12]

Opposite walls of this dramatic room were covered with fluted, extruded aluminum strips, anodized in a range of blues and purples. The back wall was covered in electric-blue Thaibok silk, and the chairs, designed by Finn Juhl, had slightly modified armrests and were trimmed in the same fabric as the wall. The carpet was black and charcoal with blue metallic Lurex threads, a static electricity inhibitor. At Earl's seat there was a control panel for music, lighting, and drapery, as well as waitstaff call buttons. The ceiling was composed of teak hexagons placed on a slightly curved dropped plane with unique hexagonal lights.[13]

For the executive offices, Knoll worked directly with Carl Benkert to specify wood and marble types, finishes, and hardware details. The desks and credenzas were mostly walnut, and the drawer units were modular solid wood boxes. Custom privacy panels for the desks were etched plastic or fabric-covered wood. Hans Knoll directed the manufacturing of all this unique furniture. Florence Knoll later wrote to George Moon with her recollections of this important GM relationship:

above
Rendering of a Technical Center executive office by Gere Kavanaugh, early 1950s

opposite top
Table in Styling executive dining room, late 1950s

opposite bottom left
Administrator's desk in executive office, ca. 1956

opposite bottom right
Credenza, late 1950s

It seems a long time ago that we worked on Eero's General Motors buildings. Those were very exciting days of development, and it was such a thrill for a young company like Knoll to have the opportunity to work on what in those days was a huge job. The chair we called the "GM" chair at the time is still in production and still looks great. I saw it on the cover of some interior design magazine just recently.[14]

With its large open spaces and wide vistas, the Technical Center was conceived to be visually appreciated from a car. As Eero remarked, "The Center was, of course, designed at automobile scale and the changing vistas were conceived to be seen as one drove around the campus."[15]

Eero worked closely with landscape architect Thomas Dolliver Church, a designer of more than two thousand gardens, widely considered the founder of the modern American garden.[16] Together they employed simple visual landscape devices such as the placement of single and double rows of trees along the roads, single rows of trees along building facades, and a perimeter forest.

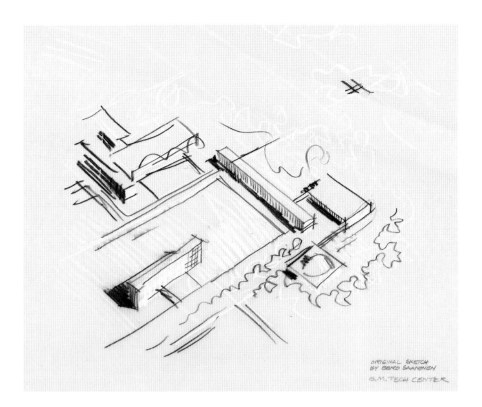

These placements create direction and movement that organize the collection of buildings into a single, cohesive environment. Within this larger design are smaller courtyards shaped by the placement of individual buildings, which serve as visual connectors to the outside. The intention of the landscape design was to unify the Technical Center while at the same time incorporating variety through uniquely planned vistas, water features, and contrasts between open and heavily planted spaces.

The buildings mirror this interplay while always maintaining a horizontal feeling. Their interconnections radiate, with each element responding to the next in a natural and simple rhythm. The systems approach, based on the five-foot module for the interior Hauserman systems and ceiling structures, facilitated the deployment of repeated rectangular shapes that relate to the curtain wall structure and out to the exterior building grid. The landscape further accentuates that low-slung aesthetic, defining the campus's organization in relation to the rectangular artificial lake. Aerial photography illustrates this interplay of shapes and ideas at the largest scale. Eero's earliest design sketch captures the essence of his concept in surprisingly intuitive and minimal gestural strokes. It provides a profound lesson in understanding his commitment to the initial conceptual ideal and its responsive outcome:

> I think of architecture as the total of man's man-made physical surroundings. The only thing I leave out is nature. You might say it is man-made nature. It is the total of everything we have around us, starting with the largest city plan, including the streets we drive on and its telephone poles and signs, down to the building and house we work and live in and does not end until we consider the chair we sit in and the ash tray we dump our pipe in. It is true that the architect practices on only a narrow segment of this wide keyboard, but that is just a matter of historical accident. The total scope is much wider than what he has staked his claim on. So to the question, what is the scope of architecture? I would answer: It is man's total physical surroundings, outdoors and indoors.[17]

above
Sketch by Eero Saarinen, 1949

overleaf
Process Development building, as seen from interior of the Engineering building, late 1950s

Research complex exterior, 1955

above
Research complex exterior with
Research Services building on the
left and Research Metallurgy building
on the right, 1955

overleaf
Lobby of the Research
administration building, 1955

above
Lobby of the Engineering
administration building, 1951

opposite
Styling auditorium interior wall,
May 22, 2015

overleaf
Canopy entrance and lobby of
the Engineering administration
building, late 1950s

previous
View from the lobby of the
Engineering administration
building, late 1950s

above
Lobby of the Process Development
administration building, 1956

136

Lobby of the Styling administration
building, late 1950s

Executive office area of the Research
administration building, ca. 1955

North entry doors of the color studio
in the Styling administration building
and floating staircase in lobby,
April 27, 1959

140

above
Executive office in the Styling
administration building, late 1950s

opposite
Executive office reception area in the
Styling administration building, 1957

overleaf
Executive dining room in Styling
administration building, featuring
untitled giclée print on brushed
aluminum by Susan Skarsgard, 2007

above
Chair designed by Finn Juhl,
upholstered in fabric designed by
Alexander Girard, in Harley Earl's
office in the Styling administration
building, 1957

opposite
Bette Hardin in Harley Earl's office,
September 10, 1957

overleaf
Cafeteria in the Styling
administration building,
May 11, 2013

opposite
Research administration
building interior, 2018

above
Basement cafeteria in the
Research administration building,
November 11, 1955

Research administration
building library, 1965

Left to right: designers Dagmar
Arnold, Tom Bradley, and
Jayne Van Alstyne with unidentified
man in the corridor of the
Styling administration building,
March 12, 1956

Styling administration
building library, 1962

Research administration building
corridor, first floor, 2005

above
Research administration building
corridor, second floor, 2018

overleaf
Exterior glazed-brick walls,
July 26, 2013

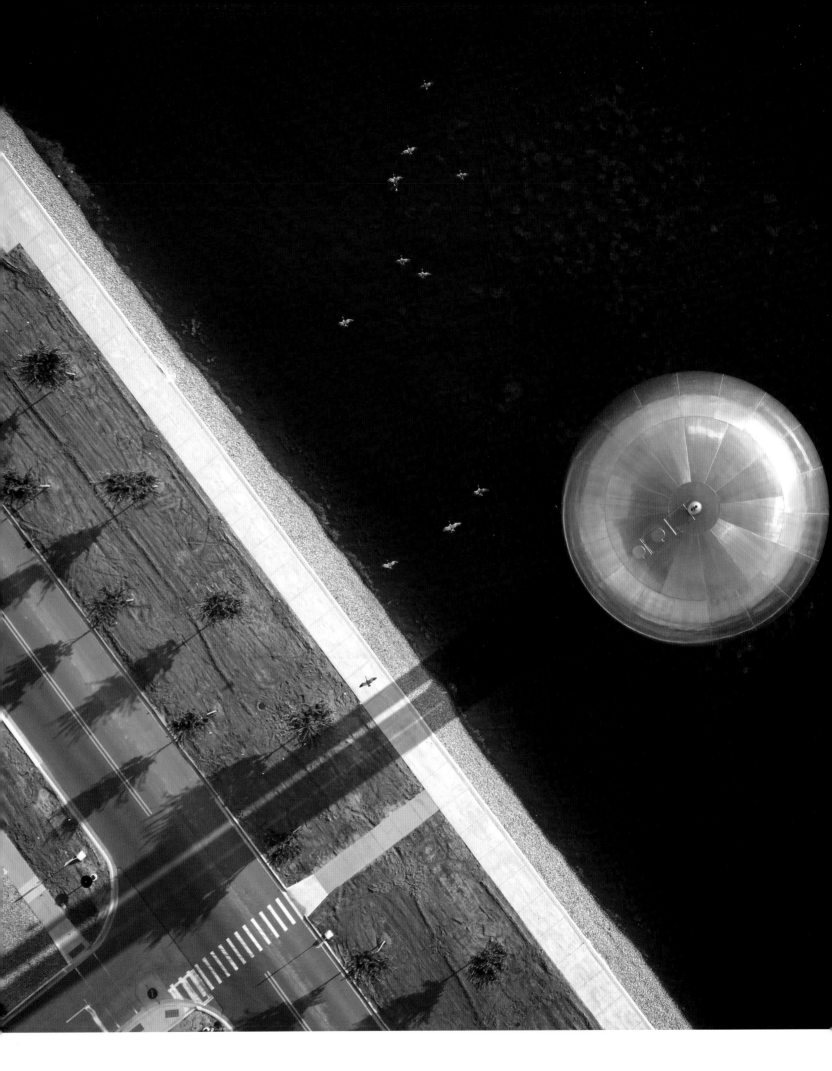

previous
Entrance canopy of the Research
administration building, 2018

left
Aerial view of water tower,
August 14, 2017

Contrast and Juxtaposition

opposite
Styling auditorium, October 21, 1955

top
Water tower, ca. 1952

bottom
Interior stairway, March 24, 2005

Eero Saarinen employed a number of elements to act as foils to the campus's "controlled rhythm of high and low buildings, of glass walls and brick walls, of buildings seen between trees and buildings open to the square."[1] Those elements were bound together by juxtapositions of scale, color, shape, and form:

> Our basic design allowed variety within unity.... Color is not used in small ways on the exterior. The brilliant blues, reds, yellow, orange, black are on the great big end walls of buildings. Some of these are about forty feet high and each is of one color, so they are rather like cards of color in space.... In the earlier scheme, there was a tall administration building which gave the project a strong, vertical focal point. When that building was dropped from the program, we sought vertical focal points in other ways. Where the administration building would have been, we put the great fountain, a 115-foot-wide, fifty-foot-high wall of moving water. Then, instead of hiding the water tower, we designed it to be a proud 132-foot-high, stainless-steel-clad spherical shape and set it in the pool as a vertical accent in the whole composition. The water ballet with its playing jets, by Alexander Calder, is another visual accent near the Research building.[2]

Focal points appear in forms both large and small. The iconic dome of the Styling auditorium is perhaps the most prominent example of this strategy. Kevin Roche came up with the idea for the aluminum-clad building; John Dinkeloo engineered it in collaboration with Smith, Hinchman & Grylls (SH&G); and the Chicago Bridge & Iron Company built it.[3] Every other building on campus speaks to the same tailored, orthogonal aesthetic and as such supports the dome-shaped building as a dramatic statement of wonder and precision in industry. Many vertical elements throughout are curvilinear, fabricated with special materials or given strong coloration. The largest of these is the water tower, situated diagonally across from the dome. In Saarinen's eyes, this functional tower was a key focal element that fit his ideal of the well-made American form, clad in stainless steel—the material of the automobile.

The staircases are another element that Saarinen designed to delight the viewer. Even the most pedestrian back stair is a minimalist work of art. But in the lobbies of three administrative buildings, the stairways are bold design statements. The one in the Service building is simple and elegant, with open risers offering an unobstructed view through the slabs of one-inch travertine set in grout on the welded steel grating. It is supported by a steel I beam with brackets that create a floating effect. This is in distinct contrast to the grand staircases in the administration building lobbies of Research and Styling, which were designed by Kevin Roche, John Dinkeloo, and SH&G. Radical in design and execution, they illustrate the collaborative convergence of engineering and

design talent present in the Detroit area at the time. The recollections of SH&G structural engineer Peter Petkoff were recorded by George Moon:

> "The most wonderful experience with Kevin was working on the staircases!" Peter reflected, on the care and energy that Kevin applied to solving these intricate design and structural problems…where the structure and the materials are the essence of the design. Pete felt that whatever Kevin tried to accomplish he worked to achieve…with a special dedication. The staircases were a constant subject in conversation with Pete Petkoff, for they epitomized, to him, the innovation and creativeness of the Saarinen office, and the successful marriage of that architectural invention with the realities of structure and mechanics, the coming-together of disciplines as well as personalities and principles.[4]

Both staircases posed intricate design and engineering problems, which were met with structural invention and creative problem solving, to extraordinary result. Each is suspended by pencil-thin tension rods secured to the floor and ceiling with polished marine hardware connectors.[5]

But that is perhaps all they have in common. The Research staircase is set at the back of the lobby, dramatically pulling the viewer into the space and up a three-stair rise toward the circular stairs. The lobby ceiling is made from walnut-veneer plywood squares, each pressed with a circle using the process developed by Charles Eames for his molded plywood furniture.[6] A beautiful, simple round desk designed by the Saarinen office resonates with the other circular details. The grand staircase reaches up through the walnut-veneer

top left
Lobby of the Research administration
building, ca. 1960

top right
Lobby ceiling of the Research
administration building, 2018

bottom
"Teacup" desk in lobby of the Styling
administration building, 1956

ceiling to the second floor through a circular opening. Twenty-three five-inch-thick black-green emerald Norwegian granite treads, weighing approximately fifteen hundred pounds each, are suspended by an ingenious attachment that functions much like spokes that form a converging cone to a hub on a bicycle wheel. The entire lobby is a symphony of contrast and juxtaposition.

The staircase in the lobby of the Styling administration building floats over a pool of water and is the most monumental visual element in this broad, rectilinear space. The switchback suspended stair is composed of travertine treads supported by polished metal rods that run from the second floor to the pool below. Beyond a wall mural, a circular, white fiberglass "teacup" desk provides a contrasting element to the staircase. Kevin Roche described the process of designing the desk:

> I did a drawing of it and…we were working with Smith, Hinchman & Grylls, so everything that we did passed over to them.…I did a cross section and plan cross section, elevation, and the detail of it…, where the receptionist would sit and how much room she'd have. I was worried about her not having enough space with the curve [at the bottom]—not having enough space for her legs… so, it was interesting.[7]

opposite
Nancy Crawford and Gerald Lockhart
in the lobby stairwell of the Styling
administration building, ca. 1956

above
Jeanette Linder (standing) and
Ruth Glennie (seated) in the color
studio with the Dupont Classified
Color Selector, 1956

overleaf
Designers in the color studio,
ca. 1956

Styling administration building
color studio, featuring *Impetus* by
James McCormick, fiberglass
and metal, undated

Perhaps the most unique room at the Technical Center is the color studio on the second floor of the Styling administration building. The donut-shaped room is another stunning example of contrasting forms creating a focal point. It is surrounded with floor-to-ceiling windows that look onto an external garden as well as, originally, an internal pool with a fountain. These features provided natural light from every direction, a detail that is as practical for the designers inhabiting the space as it is aesthetically pleasing. The room's most remarkable feature was the Dupont Classified Color Selector, a system for specifying paint color consisting of 3,488 four-by-six-inch color panels held in a display that rotated with the press of a button. (The Color Selector and internal pool area were later destroyed in a fire and not restored.) Maija Grotell, the ceramicist at Cranbrook, created a series of whimsical, boat-shaped pottery planters on chrome posts to surround the pool.[8] A round space within the room, covered with polished dimensional panels, enclosed the color evaluation room, where special lights allowed for various lighting conditions.

Eero believed in the integration of art into architecture and commissioned many artworks to be placed around the campus for visual interest and cultural engagement. His second wife, Aline Bernstein (Louchheim) Saarinen, was an art critic and television journalist in New York, and she lent her expertise and connections to the selection of artists for the Technical Center.[9]

Alexander Calder created a water feature that functioned as a large virtual mobile sculpture just outside the Research lobby in the northwest corner of the lake. Titled *Fantails, Seven Sisters, Plops and Scissors* (but commonly called the *Water Ballet* fountain), it features twenty-one jets pumping thirty-six hundred gallons per minute, shooting water forty feet high with variable pressure, which affects its speed and sound.[10] At night it is illuminated by red, yellow, and blue colored lights below the water's surface.

The first-ever large commission given to Harry Bertoia, a Cranbrook colleague of Eero's, was to design a decorative screen for the Central Restaurant. He described the experience in an interview with Paul Cummings for the Archives of American Art:

Eero Saarinen had asked me to do something for the new Technical Center building in Warren, Michigan, for General Motors, and he was the first one who really risked asking me to do something in that scale. I was unknown and untried, but he knew me personally and he probably knew what he might expect.[11]

above
Water Ballet by Alexander Calder
and water tower, 1970s

overleaf
Exterior view, Central Restaurant,
with untitled decorative wall
sculpture by Harry Bertoia, enameling
steel, late 1950s

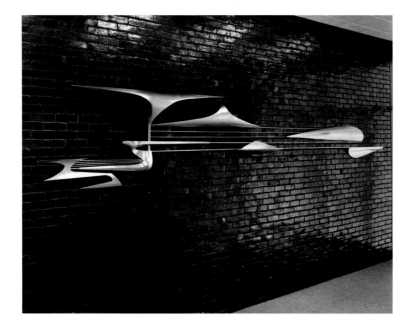

The screen, arranged in two vertical planes measuring thirty-six feet long and ten feet high, separates the entrance from the raised dining area above, providing an ornamental and visually melodic definition to the structure. The metal sculpture is made up of rectangles and squares varying in size from five to ten inches, with a thickness of one-eighth inch, supported by a grid of horizontal and vertical rods. The steel plates were enameled and then coated with metals applied in their molten state. GM was billed $18,500 for the screen.[12] A larger version of it was later commissioned for the Manufacturers Trust Company building on Fifth Avenue in New York. The Central Restaurant won the AIA Honor Award in 1955.[13]

There were several art commissions for Research, including a wonderful work by Charles Sheeler. In 1955 Sheeler visited the campus to study the Research building as he developed his idea. The painting depicts abstracted views of the iconic spiral staircase in the lobby and also illustrates technological innovations such as the Helmholtz coil (a device consisting of two electromagnets on the same axis that produce a nearly uniform magnetic field, named after the German physicist Hermann von Helmholtz) and the Dodrill-GMR mechanical heart (developed by GM Research in collaboration with Harper Hospital in Detroit, used in the first successful open-heart surgery). Sheeler received $4,500 for the painting, titled *General Motors Research*, which took six months to complete and originally hung in the executive conference room. It was Sheeler's last commissioned work.[14] For the Research executive suite lobby, a lively and vibrant oil painting by Jimmy Ernst titled *Contemporary Abstract* was selected. A portrait of Charles Kettering by Thomas E. Stephens was also commissioned.

left
The Flight of the Bird, also known as *Bird in Flight*, by Antoine Pevsner, oxidized bronze sculpture, May 1, 1956

right
Power and Direction by Gwen Lux, brushed and polished chrome sculpture, ca. 1956

Outside the Styling administration building lobby stands an extraordinary twenty-foot-high sculpture by French sculptor Antoine Pevsner titled *The Flight of the Bird*.[15] It was cast in thin-walled bronze in the same Paris foundry that made the Statue of Liberty.[16] Aline Saarinen described how she and Eero found this artist:

> We saw the Pevsner work first as a small bronze in a Paris gallery. We both felt that in heroic size it would express something of the precision and imagination represented by the automobile history. The coppery look of the raw bronze disturbed me at first, but as I study it, I rather like it.[17]

Inside the lobby of the Styling administration building hangs a large oil portrait of Alfred Sloan by Thomas E. Stephens and a huge painted stainless steel mural by Buell Mullen that covers an entire wall. On the second floor of the administration building are two metal wall sculptures designed by Gwen Lux and Wells Squier. James McCormick Jr. designed a fiberglass and metal sculpture for the pool in the color studio. Numerous other works were selected or commissioned. Many were designed by Styling employees, including Gere Kavanaugh, who created a dimensional mural, titled *Variation on a Theme*, made of brightly colored, enameled metal shapes mounted on white canvas.

Color was used throughout the campus with creativity and thoughtfulness. *Life* magazine wrote: "Not since the fabulous palaces of the Assyrian kings has color been used for architectural effect as it has in the new General Motors Technical Center. The richly varied yet stylistically simple combination of color and form…could spark a color revolution in U.S. building practice."[18]

left
Variation on a Theme by Gere Kavanaugh, fabric and metal wall mural, ca. 1954

right
General Motors Research by Charles Sheeler, in the Research administration building, oil on canvas, 1956

Alexander Girard was the colorist for the project and selected bright and cheery colors for both function and fancy. For instance, the huge power plant stacks and equipment were painted in bright colors, coded to identify their function. The Vitra Design Museum catalog *Alexander Girard: A Designer's Universe* (2016) notes: "Pipes were painted blue, motors and valves red, and stairs and balustrades yellow. The strong primary colors reminded a journalist writing for the magazine *House & Garden* of paintings by Fernand Léger."[19]

The lively orange interior of the Styling cafeteria, designed by Warren Platner in conjunction with GM designers, is a great example of collaboration in color. Located on the third floor, it has a grand view of the campus. Its built-in circular banquette seating is upholstered in bright orange plastic, and the floor is covered with thin alternating strips of white and orange tile.[20]

The exterior glazed-brick end walls display the most iconic use of
vibrant color and texture and are certainly a dramatic rebuttal to accusations
of a Miesian influence on the campus design. Kevin Roche initially disagreed
with this use of color because it strayed from strict International Style
restraint in applied ornamentation.[21] But with time he came to see it
differently and eventually conceded that it is one of the defining features
of the Technical Center.

right
Dynamometer building
exterior, undated

overleaf
Ceiling of the Research shop
building, 2018

previous
Exterior glazed-brick wall,
May 26, 2013

above
Styling administration building lobby,
with view of "teacup" desk and *Lines
in Motion* by Buell Mullen, oil on
etched metal, undated

opposite
Lobby staircase of the Styling
administration building,
October 17, 1979

overleaf
Styling auditorium interior,
March 18, 1957

186

opposite
Process Development building
auditorium, October 21, 1955

above
Research administration
building auditorium, 2018

above
Styling building color studio, 1956

opposite
Styling building color studio fountain,
titled *Impetus*, by James McCormick,
fiberglass and metal, May 24, 1956

overleaf
Styling building color studio color
evaluation room, ca. 1956

Left to right: unknown designer,
Jeanette Krebs, and Ruth Glennie
in the color studio, color matching
room, 1956

Styling building color studio,
February 17, 1956

left
Canopy and entrance of the Styling
administration building, featuring *The
Flight of the Bird* by Antoine Pevsner,
late 1950s

overleaf
Vertical "wall of water" fountain and
Styling auditorium, 1957

opposite
Water Ballet fountain by Alexander
Calder, late 1950s

above
Styling auditorium, 1955

overleaf
Styling auditorium, July 26, 2013

above and opposite
Water tower, late 1950s

CHAPTER EIGHT

Precision and Innovation

"Architecture is like a marvelous three-dimensional chess game. Every move or decision affects every other move and decision. You have to keep thinking about and juggling all the parts at the same time. In general, if I had to say how we work...we start by considering very carefully the problem of the site, the problem of the program, and the problem of the spirit of the particular job.... Then we start gradually trying to put the answers to these problems together and then, with them, we start putting in the structural system."
—Eero Saarinen[1]

Eero Saarinen used the automobile industry as a metaphor to develop modular construction techniques that facilitated a flexible architectural assembly process, based on clear technical needs. He faced the problem of constructing modern curtain-walled buildings during an early period in the development of this type of architecture. The limitations of contemporary technology could be overcome only through collaboration and innovation. The Saarinen firm was assisted by General Motors in seeking leading-edge solutions to many of these problems. In Saarinen's words:

> One of the things we are proudest of is that, working together with General Motors, we developed many "firsts" in the building industry. I think that is part of the architect's responsibility....All of these developments have become part of the building industry and a common part of the language of modern architecture.[2]

Among the most innovative building techniques developed for the Technical Center were the neoprene rubber gaskets used to seal the panels in the curtain walls in order to make them watertight. This development allowed for a minimal profile of prefabricated extruded aluminum on the exterior faces of the buildings. The resulting grid frames the blue-green heat-absorbing glass and the porcelain enamel panels to create the signature clean, strong, graphic aesthetic of the curtain wall construction.

The use of modular elements allowed flexibility in the arrangement of interior space for the ever-changing requirements of business. These elements included the Hauserman wall system and the suspended, integrated five-foot ceiling modules for heating and ventilation. GM Styling led the development of molded, translucent plastic pans to spread light evenly without casting shadows in the design studios and offices and proclaimed it the first use of a completely luminous ceiling structure.[3] New and innovative manufacturing techniques were developed for the production of glazed brick for the distinctive end walls of various structures. The intensely colored glazed brick resulted from a collaborative investigation between the architects, their consultants, and

opposite
Oldsmobile 98 in front of the
Engineering building, June 6, 1957

above
Drafting room in Styling studio
building, ca. 1956

top
Styling studio building,
June 23, 2013

bottom left
Glazed-brick end wall behind 1960
Cadillac Series 62 four-window
sedan, 1960

bottom right
Engineering building, May 26, 2013

GM's AC Spark Plug division. This elevation of handcraft celebrates the enduring human force in industrial society.

It was the architect's vision to capture the essence and pride of industry and provide a humane and creative workplace—placid and beautiful, vibrant and dynamic, progressive and optimistic. The repeated but variable exterior rectilinear framing unifies the campus design and embodies the conceptual ideals behind it through function and form. The varying designs of the buildings' canopies provide a clear expression of the individualism of the distinct disciplines on campus. These canopies face either north or south and extend an understated and extraordinarily graceful invitation to enter the full-height, glass-enclosed lobbies. They speak to one another visually, but each is unique and of minimal design interpretation. There are no grand edifices to exalted leaders, no appropriation of extravagance from a previous style. Instead, it is a quiet architecture of carefully rendered, culturally symbolic, invented form.

The synergetic process that Eero Saarinen embraced to achieve his vision further demonstrates this confluence of intent. He wanted to design this project for the client and with the client, which set up a perfect problem-solving laboratory for functional design solutions. The Saarinen office took advantage of the rich environment of Detroit job shops supporting the auto industry to quickly prototype fixtures, attachments, and trims supportive of this new, minimal aesthetic. They also engaged designers, architects, and artists from the rich pool of talent that Detroit had to offer. Eero best described how he viewed the collaborative nature of architecture:

> Unlike painting and sculpture, where the individual works entirely alone, architecture involves many people. It is true that it has to be siphoned through one mind, but there is always teamwork.[4]

It was a convergence of the people, the place, the ideals, and the era—a moment of great significance in the development of midcentury modernism in the United States.

top
Service section building,
October 21, 1955

bottom
Lobby of the Engineering
administration building,
August 6, 1951

above
Canopy entrance of the Process
Development building with
1956 GMC 100 Series panel
truck, late 1950s

opposite
Research administration building
exterior seen from the lobby interior,
October 4, 1955

overleaf
Water tower seen from canopy
entrance of the Service section
building, October 12, 1955

Canopy entrance of the Research
administration building, 1955

1956 Pontiac in front of the
canopy entrance of the Research
administration building, May 24, 1955

above
Glass curtain wall and
glazed-brick exterior, 1955

Exterior wall and stacks,
October 4, 1955

opposite
Exterior curtain wall,
August 22, 1955

above
Service section building
exterior, 1954

223   CHAPTER EIGHT: PRECISION AND INNOVATION

opposite
Designers and modelers at work
in the GMC truck studio in the
Styling building, 1956

above
Inside the Styling shop building,
fabrication of full-size model in
wood and plaster of the 1956
Firebird II concept car, 1956

225   CHAPTER EIGHT: PRECISION AND INNOVATION

above

Research building clocks.
Top left and right: conference room;
bottom left and right: second-floor
reception area, 2018

opposite

Central Restaurant building
interior, August 2, 1957

226

above
Switchboard room in the Service
section shop building, June 25, 1952

opposite
Testing automotive lamps in
the Engineering building interior,
June 22, 1955

above
Designer Anthony Lapine
in the Styling studio building,
February 24, 1956

opposite
Designers and sculptors working
in the Styling studio building,
October 4, 1955

Aerial view of Technical Center
campus, late 1950s

The General Motors Technical Center has functioned as the epicenter of the company's global product development since it opened its doors in 1956. It is a living organism that has continued to evolve in response to the ever-changing needs of business and technology. Even before the original Saarinen campus was completed, GM directed the modification of several of the main building groups, while maintaining the overall aesthetic. GM also began to develop the east side of the campus, which is separated from the original groupings by a railroad, through its architectural division, Argonaut Realty.

Over the years, changing technical requirements have necessitated alterations to some of the structures, such as the addition of mechanical equipment on the roofs. However, it is remarkable how much the Saarinen side of the campus has remained aesthetically pure. Part of this is a testament to Eero's commitment to use the very best materials and to proactively design flexibility into the basic structures, allowing for modifications to accommodate changing business needs. This also results from GM's commitment to the campus and an understanding of its role as steward of this midcentury modern masterpiece. A profound illustration of this is the $1 billion investment for renovation and expansion that GM announced in 2015, along with a name change to the GM *Global* Technical Center, which further defines the campus's role for the future. A sensitive renovation of the Styling auditorium, or "dome," by SmithGroup was one of the first projects in this initiative; it resulted in a 2017 AIA Institute Honor Award in Interior Architecture.

In 2014 the campus was designated a National Historic Landmark by the United States Department of the Interior and the National Park Service. The nomination process involved a collaborative effort between the State of Michigan Historic Preservation Office and the GM Design Archive & Special Collections. The commendation on the plaque reads:

This site possesses national significance as one of the most important works of modernist architect Eero Saarinen. The Technical Center marks Saarinen's emergence onto the international stage as an architect, planner and designer of total environments. Begun in 1949 and dedicated in 1956, the complex set the design standard for a new concept in suburban corporate campuses.

An awareness of the architectural significance of this campus is a value that has been handed down from one generation of its inhabitants to the next. There have also been individual champions who have worked passionately to preserve this important history and to cultivate in the campus's residents an appreciation of the place and our responsibility to this American treasure. This book documents the story from our unique, inside perspective. It celebrates the lasting legacy of Eero Saarinen's design achievement for you and for the people who continue to imagine the future for General Motors.

overleaf
Styling auditorium, May 22, 2015

ACKNOWLEDGMENTS

The collaborative nature of our work environment at General Motors is reflected in every aspect of the making of this book, and as a result, there are many people to acknowledge and thank for their important contributions.

Michael Simcoe, vice president of Global Design, championed this book idea from start to finish. His engagement with the Global Design Leadership Team—John Cafaro, Helen Emsley, Sharon Gauci, Bryan Nesbitt, Ken Parkinson, Andrew Smith, and Tina Brimo—is a clear demonstration of the value our leaders place on preserving our company's history. Grateful thanks go to them and to my many colleagues who lent their considerable expertise: Robyn Henderson, Timothy Gorbatoff, Michael McBride, Tina Berry, Sandra Spires, Chuck Cloud, Candice Messing, David G. Spencer, and Camren Fair.

My colleagues in the GM Design Archive & Special Collections, GM Heritage Center, and GM Media Archive assisted me in every aspect of the production. My most profound and sincere thanks go to them for taking on this huge project with curiosity and tenacity. This includes Christo Datini, Wayne Morrical, Natalie Morath, Larry Kinsel, Shelly Joseph, and Emily Allen. This group did the heavy lifting.

I received meaningful encouragement, information, and support from former GM colleagues, including Ed Welburn, Larry Faloon, Teckla Rhoads, Craig Duprey, Delf Dodge, Mark Lennox, Pamela Waters, Dick Cruger, Michele Assad, MaryEllen Dohrs, Reginald Gay, John Rapp, Kurt Struckmeyer, Richard Mantych, Fred Overcash, and Maryanne Torner. Most important, thanks to Mark Leavy, who set me off on this road some twelve years ago and facilitated every effort to document the important history of our campus.

Along the way I have met many extraordinary individuals who had a direct relationship with the Saarinen firm; their memories and experiences were critical and added depth, veracity, and color to this story. First and foremost is Kevin Roche. In writing the foreword, he set up this story as no one else could have. I am sincerely grateful to him for sharing his inspiring recollections and generous wit. Others include Piet van Dijk, Ruth Adler Schnee, Susan Saarinen, and Eric Saarinen. Gere Kavanaugh, also a GM Design alumna, listened and offered her wise counsel and generous spirit, propelling this project forward at its most critical junctures.

I'd like to acknowledge the importance of George Moon's memoir as an invaluable resource, providing a firsthand understanding of the relationship between the Saarinen firm and GM. Thank you to his daughters, Carol Herbig and Anne Farris. Thanks also to Catherine Benkert, for sharing the archive of her father, Carl.

Grateful recognition goes to the many unnamed General Motors staff photographers for the historic imagery selected for this story, as well as to current GM photographers Thomas Drew and John Neuville for their extraordinary view of the campus today. Retouching and image processing were done by Wayne Morrical, Stephen Gray, Johnathan Schweitzer, Rodney Morr, Kathleen Tokarski, and Eric Shawl. I'd also like to acknowledge the work of the great American architectural photographers Balthazar Korab, Ezra Stoller, and Carol Highsmith. James Haefner's recent dramatic photography of the campus captures the essence of Saarinen's vision like no one else's.

Special thanks to Charles Phoenix, Diana Murphy, Mark Coir, Pierluigi Serraino, Alan Hess, and Donald Albrecht for sharing their valuable experience and advice. And to these wonderful individuals for their support and encouragement: Mark Davis, Louise Sandhaus, Diane Blumson, Maria Phillips, Sam Huszczo, Crystal Babbie Huszczo, Carole Campbell, Pavel Vasilev, Jacques Caussin, Barbara Brown, Dan Arbor, Jill Wiltse, H. Kirk Brown III, Ellen Shook, Gregory Saldana, and Jonathan Segal.

These individuals and their institutions were instrumental in research support: Linda Scinto, Roche Dinkeloo Associates; Brian Conway and Amy Arnold, State of Michigan Historic Preservation Office; Gregory Wittkopp, Gina Tecos, and Leslie Edwards, Cranbrook Archives, Cranbrook Center for Collections and Research; Kristen Chinery, Walter P. Reuther Library, Wayne

1956 Pontiac Star Chief convertible coupe
on the Technical Center campus, ca. 1956

State University; Mick Kennedy, University of Michigan, A. Alfred Taubman College of Architecture and Urban Planning; Pam Shermeyer, the *Detroit News*; Robert Dirig, ArtCenter Archives, ArtCenter College of Design; Maria Ketcham, Research Library & Archives, Detroit Institute of Arts; Jim Ottaviani, University of Michigan Library; Franc Nunoo-Quarcoo, Stamps School of Art & Design, University of Michigan; Jeff Gaines, Albert Kahn Associates; Gregory Miller, Kettering University Archives; Debbie Welsh, Allied Vaughn; Mónica Ponce de León, Princeton University School of Architecture; Archives of American Art, Smithsonian Institution; Suzanne Noruschat, University of Southern California Libraries Special Collections; Jessica Becker, Jessica Quagliaroli, Stephen Ross, and Bill Landis, Manuscripts & Archives, Yale University Library; Heather Gendron, Robert B. Haas Family Arts Library, Yale University Library.

Finally, my most grateful thanks go to the staff at Princeton Architectural Press. Abby Bussel led the way by acquiring the project and patiently walking me through the initial editorial process to form this story. Sara Stemen edited and refined this into a coherent narrative and guided me through the production process with kindness and supreme competence. I am especially grateful to Paul Wagner for his beautiful design that allows the architecture itself to visually tell the story. Thanks also to Kevin Lippert, publisher; Janet Behning, production director; Valerie Kamen, prepress coordinator; Lia Hunt, sales and marketing director; and Wes Seeley, publicity manager. I cannot thank them enough for their engagement and partnership.

DEDICATION GREETINGS

FROM THE **BUILDERS** OF THE

GENERAL MOTORS TECHNICAL CENTER

25 BUILDINGS ON 300-ACRE SITE

EERO SAARINEN & ASSOCIATES
Architects

BRYANT & DETWILER COMPANY
General Contractors
ESTABLISHED IN 1906

SMITH, HINCHMAN & GRYLLS, INC.
Architects & Engineers

Company	Work	Company	Work	Company	Work
AMERICAN BRIDGE COMPANY	Structural Steel	W. D. GALE, INC.	Electrical Work	J. LIVINGSTON & CO., INC.	Electrical Work
BROOKER ELECTRIC CO., INC.	Electrical Work	GENERAL BRONZE CORPORATION	Ornamental Metal	LORNE PLUMBING & HEATING CO.	Mechanical Work
CHICAGO BRIDGE & IRON CO.	Auditorium Dome	JOHN E. GREEN PLUMBING & HEATING CO.	Mechanical Work	MOYNAHAN BRONZE CO., INC.	Ornamental Metal
DENTON CONSTRUCTION CO.	Road Paving	THE F. F. HAUSERMAN CO.	Metal Partitions	CHAS. J. ROGERS, INC.	Excavation
DRAKE AVERY COMPANY	Mechanical Work	ROBERT HUTTON & CO., INC.	Roofing and Sheet Metal	THE STANLEY-CARTER CO.	Mechanical Work
ENGINEERING METAL PRODUCTS CORP.	Miscellaneous Metal	HYDON-BRAND COMPANY	Electrical Work	THERMOTANK INC.	Air Conditioning
THE FARRINGTON COMPANY	Mechanical Work	INGRAM IRON WORKS, INC.	Miscellaneous Metal	TURNER-BROOKS, INC.	Resilient Flooring
FLOUR CITY ORNAMENTAL IRON CO.	Ornamental Metal	JOHNSON, LARSEN & CO.	Mechanical Work	WOLVERINE PORCELAIN ENAMEL CO.	Porcelain Enamel Panels

Company	Work	Company	Work	Company	Work
ALLIED STEEL & CONVEYORS, INC.	Miscellaneous Metal	GIBRALTER FLOORS, INC.	Tile and Terrazzo	OTIS ELEVATOR COMPANY	Elevators
ALUMINUM & ARCHITECTURAL METALS CO.	Ornamental Metal	GLANZ & KILLIAN COMPANY	Fire Protection System	POM-McFATE COMPANY	Cabinet Work
BABCOCK & WILCOX COMPANY	Steam Generating Units	JOS. M. HUGHES & SONS	Excavation	JOS. SCHAFER COMPANY	Painting
THE JOHN H. BUSBY COMPANY	Electrical Work	THE R. C. MAHON COMPANY	Steel Decking	SCHROEDER PAINT & GLASS CO.	Glass and Glazing
BYRNE DOORS, INC.	Vertical Lift Doors	R. H. McMANUS & CO.	Sewer Systems	R. L. SPITZLEY HEATING CO.	Mechanical Work
CADILLAC GLASS COMPANY	Glass and Glazing	MECHANICAL HEAT & COLD, INC.	Mechanical Work	THE STEARNS COMPANY	Kitchen Equipment
DAVIS BROS., INC.	Steam Fitting Trades Work	A. J. MILLER, INC.	Lawn Irrigation	TOLEDO PLATE & WINDOW GLASS CO.	Glass and Glazing
FENESTRA, INC.	Steel Windows	MOTOR CITY ELECTRIC CO.	Electrical Work	THE W. E. TURLEY COMPANY	Cabinet Work
GABRIEL STEEL COMPANY	Steel Framing	NARDONI CEMENT FLOOR CO.	Cement Finish	WESTERN WATERPROOFING CO.	Metallic Waterproofing
LOUIS GARAVAGLIA	Asphalt Surfacing	NEWMAN BROTHERS, INC.	Ornamental Metal	WHITCOMB-BAUER FLOORING, INC.	Wood Flooring

Company	Work	Company	Work	Company	Work
ACE SPRINKLER COMPANY	Fire Protection System	GLOBE AUTOMATIC SPRINKLER CO.	Fire Protection System	THE NICHOLS COMPANY	Acoustic Tile
ACME ELEVATOR COMPANY	Hydraulic Elevator	GLOBE HOIST COMPANY	Freight Elevator	NUKEM PRODUCTS CORP.	Acid Brick Floors
ACME WIRE & IRON WORKS	Metal Toilet Stalls	JOHN L. GOSS CORPORATION	Granite	OHIO PLATE GLASS COMPANY	Glass and Glazing
ACORN IRON WORKS, INC.	Structural Steel	GRAY ELECTRIC CO.	Electrical Work	E. H. O'NEILL FLOOR CO.	Sparkproof Floors
AETNA STEEL PRODUCTS CORP.	Hollow Metal	HALL ENGINEERING COMPANY	Electrical Work	A. L. OPPENHEIMER CO.	Steel Fire Doors
ALLIED LEAD CONSTRUCTION CO.	X-Ray Insulation	N. W. HAMILL COMPANY	Hollow Metal	ORNAMENTAL IRON WORK CO.	Ornamental Metal
ALLIED PAINTING & DECORATING CO.	Painting	HANNA, ZABRISKIE & DARON	Gunite Work	THE C. J. PAGE TILE CO.	Tile Work
AMERICAN ROOFING COMPANY	Roofing and Sheet Metal	HARNISCHFEGER CORPORATION	Cranes	L. PALOMBIT TILE COMPANY	Tile and Terrazzo
ANCHOR STEEL & CONVEYOR CO.	Turntables	R. V. HARTY CO., INC.	Turn-Over Door	PARMENTER STEEL & CONVEYOR CO.	Cranes
ART METAL CONSTRUCTION CO.	Hollow Metal	HAUGHTON ELEVATOR COMPANY	Elevators	THE PEELLE COMPANY	Soundproof Doors
AUSTIN'S	Painting	HAVEN-BUSCH COMPANY	Miscellaneous Metal	HARRY S. PETERSON CO.	Caulking
AUTOMATIC SPRINKLER CORP. OF AMERICA	Fire Protection System	HEINEMAN & LOVETT CO.	Metallic Waterproofing	ALBERT PICK CO., INC.	Kitchen Equipment
BERGER MFG. COMPANY	Steel Lockers	MARTIN HOFFMAN COMPANY	Porcelain Enamel Panels	RAYMOND CONCRETE PILE CO.	Piling
BERTI PLASTERING COMPANY	Lathing and Plastering	C. T. HOGAN & COMPANY, INC.	Cold Room Insulation	REICHLE SONS COMPANY	Kitchen Equipment
JULIUS BING SAFE CO.	Vault Door	HOPE'S WINDOWS, INC.	Steel Windows	RIC-WIL COMPANY	Corrosion Protection
BROWN & RAISCH COMPANY	Structural Granite	THE J. L. HUDSON COMPANY	Venetian Blinds	RICHARDS-WILCOX MFG. CO.	Metal Folding Doors
BRUNY BROTHERS	Tile and Terrazzo	ITALIAN MOSAIC & TILE CO.	Tile and Terrazzo	ROBBIE ROBINSON COMPANY	X-Ray Insulation
PHILIP CAREY MFG. COMPANY	Roofing and Sheet Metal	JAMESTOWN METAL CORP.	Hollow Metal	ROCKWOOD SPRINKLER CO.	Fire Protection System
ARMOND CASSIL, INC.	Railroad Siding	JED PRODUCTS COMPANY	Automatic Doors	ROTARY LIFT COMPANY	Freight Elevators
CHAFFEE ROOFING COMPANY	Roofing and Sheet Metal	JENNISON-WRIGHT CORP.	Wood Block Flooring	RUSLANDER & SONS, INC.	Kitchen Equipment
CINCINNATI FLOOR CO., INC.	Wood Flooring	JENNITE PRODUCTS, INC.	Coating of Pavements	MICHAEL A. SANTORO	Lathing and Plastering
CYCLONE FENCE COMPANY	Fence Work	JOHNS-MANVILLE SALES CORP.	Acoustic Ceilings	SAUNDERS & COMPANY	Industrial Steel Doors
N. DeCAMPLE COMPANY	Lathing and Plastering	KALMAN FLOOR CO., INC.	Cement Finish	SCHREIBER ROOFING COMPANY	Roofing and Sheet Metal
WILLIAM DIEDRICH COMPANY	Painting	KEWAUNEE MFG. COMPANY	Laboratory Equipment	SERVICE ART PLASTERING CO.	Lathing and Plastering
DETROIT CONCRETE PRODUCTS CORP.	Parking Lot Paving	WALTER KIDDE & CO., INC.	Fire Protection System	CHAS. SEXAUER ROOFING CO.	Roofing & Sheet Metal
DETROIT ELEVATOR COMPANY	Turntable Lift	R. E. LEGGETTE COMPANY	Metal Toilet Stalls	SOUTHEASTERN ELECTRIC CO., INC.	Electrical Work
DETROIT FIBERGLAS INSULATION CO.	Acoustic Ceilings	MAUL MACOTTA CORP.	Macotta	A. E. SPARLING COMPANY	Hydraulic Lift
DETROIT INDEPENDENT SPRINKLER CO.	Fire Protection System	McNULTY BROS. COMPANY	Lathing and Plastering	SPRAY-COAT INCORPORATED	Corrosion Protection
DETROIT MARBLE COMPANY	Marble	MESKER BROS. IRON CO.	Steel Windows	SUGDEN & SIVIER, INC.	Excavation
DETROIT ROLLING DOOR CO.	Folding Partitions	MICHCORK COMPANY	Cork Insulation	TAYLOR & GASKIN, INC.	Miscellaneous Metal
EAMES & BROWN, INC.	Painting	THE MILLS COMPANY	Metal Toilet Stalls	TRUSCON STEEL COMPANY	Steel Windows
ELEVATOR CONSTRUCTION & SERVICE CO.	Freight Elevators	MODERNFOLD DOOR SALES CO.	Folding Partitions	VIKING SPRINKLER CO.	Fire Protection System
FIREBAR DOORS, INC.	Soundproof Doors	JAMES A. MOYNES & CO.	Cabinet Work	W. BIDDLE WALKER CO.	Metal Decking and Siding
JOHN H. FREEMAN COMPANY	Finish Hardware	MUNZ SPRALAWN SYSTEMS	Lawn Irrigation	WILLIAMSBURG STEEL PRODUCTS CORP.	Hollow Metal
				WOLVERINE MARBLE COMPANY	Marble

Saarinen and Associates; Smith, Hinchman &
Grylls, Inc.; and Bryant & Detwiler Company
acknowledged the builders involved in the
GM Technical Center project in this full-page
advertisement published in a special section of
the *Detroit News*, May 15, 1956.

Eero Saarinen on the General Motors Technical Center

Our intention was threefold: to provide the best possible facilities for industrial research; to create a unified, beautiful, and human environment; and to find an appropriate architectural expression.

General Motors is a metal-working industry; it is a precision industry; it is a mass-production industry. All these things should, in a sense, be expressed in the architecture of its Technical Center.

Thus, the design is based on steel—the metal of the automobile. Like the automobile itself, the buildings are essentially put together, as on an assembly line, out of mass-produced units. And, down to the smallest detail, we tried to give the architecture the precise, well-made look which is a proud characteristic of industrial America. The architecture attempts to find its eloquence out of a consistent and logical development of its industrial character. It has been said that in these buildings I was very much influenced by Mies. But this architecture really carries forward the tradition of American factory buildings which had its roots in the Middle West in the early automobile factories of Albert Kahn.

Maximum flexibility was a prime requirement of the complicated program. It was achieved by applying the five-foot module not only to steel construction but also to laboratory, heating, ventilating, and fire-protection facilities as well as to laboratory furniture, storage units, wall partitions, and so on, all of which are keyed to it.

Now, as to the environment. The site occupies the central 320 acres of an approximately 900-acre area. The Center consists of five separate staff organizations—Research, Process Development, Engineering, Styling, and a Service Center as well as a central restaurant (in addition to cafeterias in the building groups). Each staff organization has its own constellation of buildings. There are twenty-five of these, including laboratory, office and shop buildings, and special use ones, like the two Dynamometer buildings.

Some sort of campus plan seemed right, but we were concerned with the problem of achieving an architectural unity with these horizontal buildings. The earlier scheme we made in 1945 had its great terrace and covered walk which unified the buildings into one great enterprise, but these had proved expensive and impractical. In the new scheme, developed when General Motors came back in 1948, we depended on simpler visual devices.

One of these is the twenty-two-acre pool. Not only does this form one dominant open space, but it also helps unity by providing a strong, hard architectural line and by strengthening all vertical dimensions of the buildings through their reflection.

Another unifying device is the surrounding forest, the green belt that should in time give the buildings the effect of being placed on the edge of a large glen. We gave very careful study to the placing and heights of the various buildings so they would form a controlled rhythm of high and low buildings, of glass walls and brick walls, of buildings seen between trees and buildings open to the square. Our basic design allowed variety within unity. The standardization of module throughout the project was arrived at for practical reasons, but we also hoped the constant use of this one dimension would have a unifying effect.

The use of color in an overall sense was devised, not only for its pleasing aspects, but also to help bind the project together. By an overall sense, I mean that color is not used in small ways on the exterior. The brilliant blues, reds, yellow, orange, black are on the great big end walls of buildings. Some of these are about forty feet high and each is of one color, so they are rather like cards of color in space. Then all the glass and metal walls have certain standardized neutral colors.

In the earlier scheme, there was a tall administration building which gave the project a strong, vertical focal point. When that building was dropped from the program, we sought vertical focal points in other ways. Where the administration building would have been, we put the great fountain, a 115-foot-wide, fifty-foot-high wall of moving water. Then, instead of hiding the water tower, we designed it to be a proud 132-foot-high, stainless-steel-clad spherical shape and set it in the pool as a vertical accent in the whole composition. The water ballet with its playing jets, by Alexander Calder, is another visual accent near the Research building.

The Center was, of course, designed at automobile scale and the changing vistas were conceived to be seen as one drove around the project. However, opposite the water wall fountain, in front of the central restaurant, we deliberately created a little pedestrian-scale court.

Each of the staff organizations prides itself on its own individuality and its range of activities. Each wanted its own "personality." We tried to answer this desire architecturally in the main lobby of each of the five groups. In four of these,

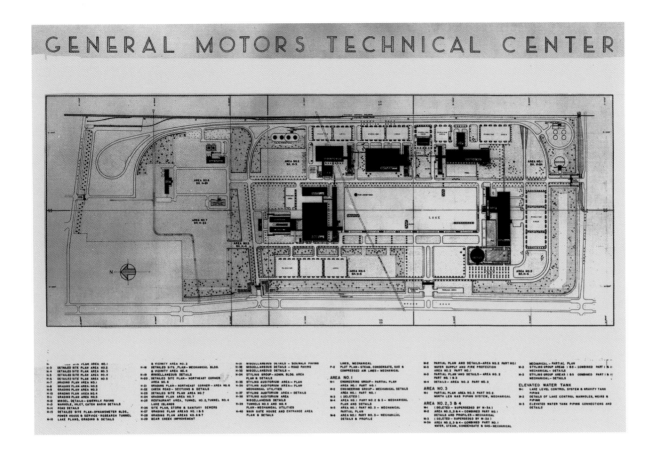

GENERAL MOTORS TECHNICAL CENTER

the visual climax to the lobby is the main staircase. These staircases are deliberately made into ornamental elements, like large-scale technological sculptures.

The public usually does not see the shop areas of the Center. We tried to keep the architectural character of the whole. They are generally wonderfully big open areas with long-span construction. We organized all the mechanical facilities with the structure so that we could avoid the usual slum-like appearance of factory buildings. We used color on the machines to make the areas visually agreeable and to unify them in the total environment. In the Dynamometer buildings, the free-standing exhaust pipes were designed to be strong elements in the composition.

One of the things we are proudest of is that, working together with General Motors, we developed many "firsts" in the building industry. I think that this is part of the architect's responsibility.

We had previously used a baked enamel-finished panel on the Pharmacy Building at Drake University, which may well have been the very first instance of the now so familiar metal curtain wall. But General Motors represents the first significant installation of laminated panels and the first use anywhere of a uniquely thin porcelain-faced sandwich panel which is a complete prefabricated wall for both exterior and interior. For this project, we also developed the brilliantly colored glazed brick. The ceilings in the drafting rooms are the first developed completely luminous ceilings using special modular plastic

pans. Perhaps the greatest gift to the building industry is the development of the neoprene gasket weather seal, which holds fixed glass and porcelain enamel metal panels to their aluminum frames. It is truly windproof and waterproof and is capable of allowing the glass or panels to be "zipped out" whenever a building's use changes. All of these developments have become part of the building industry and a common part of the language of modern architecture. [1949–1957, *passim*]

Every time I go to the Tech Center, I think what a great client General Motors was. The buildings are perfectly maintained. And they prove that in the long run good materials pay. The Engineering group is eight years old, but it looks as if it had been finished yesterday. [January 25, 1961]

From *Eero Saarinen on His Work: A Selection of Buildings Dating from 1947 to 1964 with Statements by the Architect*, ed. Aline B. Saarinen (New Haven and London: Yale University Press, 1962)

above
Map of GM Technical Center,
February 1, 1956

THE GREATEST FRONTIER

REMARKS AT THE **DEDICATION PROGRAM**
GENERAL MOTORS TECHNICAL CENTER

RECEIVED
JUN 5 1956
SALES DEPT.

Detroit, Michigan, May 16, 1956

Mr. Curtice

And now, ladies and gentlemen, the President of the United States.

The Rich Reward Ahead
by
The President of the United States
Dwight D. Eisenhower

Members of the General Motors family: It is truly an honor to participate with you today in this dedication of this new and great research center of America. It is a new adventure for frontiersmen. The history of America is a history of frontiers, and each frontier has been a challenge to Americans to dare more, to do more, to go forward faster and on a broader front.

We had geographical frontiers, always lying out there in the West and the Appalachians, challenging every person that was an inhabitant of those first thirteen Colonies. And so we had Lewis and Clark, and Pike, and all the rest opening up that great country. Even today some of those frontiers still remain. And we have great and gallant Americans exploring the Antarctic and the Arctic. Always a frontier—the challenge—and the response.

We had our economic frontiers. We started as a nation of small farms and little shops when the fur trade was in its infancy. And we learned about the gold in California; we learned about the great expanse of the West where we could raise cattle and produce our food. Frontiersmen went into them. We built roads and railroads to open up all those lands. Inventors came along and we had great machines to meet our needs. And so we had the great economic revolution of the nineteenth and twentieth centuries that has so changed our lives.

We were a nation of political frontiersmen. The reason that today we so admire Franklin and Washington and Patrick Henry—Jefferson, Lincoln, is because they dared to think new thoughts about the way that men should govern themselves—the institutions and the procedures they should set up—and devised a scheme that has stood the test of time and has met our need for progress, with men enjoying equal justice, rights, and the great opportunities.

So it might be said that the frontiersman is symbolic of the United States. General Motors was founded by frontiersmen, people who were not satisfied with what we had and were determined to make it possible for men to travel faster and better and in greater comfort. Among those frontiersmen, two of your greatest were, of course, Alfred Sloan, Jr. and Mr. Kettering. Their accomplishments were so great in the technological field that today their names are household words in

25

our country. Even since they have at least partially laid aside their work in that regard, they are still frontiersmen, showing us all how duties and citizenship can better be performed, how men can better discharge their duties in this country as citizens.

Here with me today is another frontiersman. I just had lunch with him—the President of the great country of Indonesia. America is honored that President Sukarno has come to visit us. He wants to see, among other things, this great research center you are establishing, and he is going to visit you on May twenty-eighth.

This particular Center is a place for leadership in furthering new attacks on the technological frontier. Beyond that frontier lie better and fuller employment, opportunities for people to demonstrate yet again the value of a system based on the dignity of the human being, and on their free opportunities in life.

Beyond it lie people, better capable of working with others and so that they may share what they learn with our friends in the world.

We hope that we will be fortunate enough to be able to give President Sukarno something that he may carry to his people. We would be very proud indeed if he should find something here worth while carrying back.

So in this technological center, we have this development of new machines responding in their efficiency to the constantly inquiring mind of the technician, that they in turn will produce yet broader freedoms and richer dignity for human beings, more rewarding lives, for all America and we hope through all the world.

So now, as I say goodbye, good luck to each of you, let me wish every success to this new technological center of General Motors.

27

30

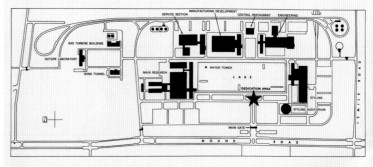

The Greatest Frontier, a booklet compiled and published by GM to commemorate the Technical Center dedication, features photographs and reprints of speeches from the event, 1956

Chicago Bridge & Iron Company on the design and construction of the water tower

The tank is used to augment the municipal water supply and insure dependable gravity water pressure to comply with fire regulations.

The plates used in the construction of the tank are Type 304 stainless clad on A-283 Grade-C steel and produced a strikingly beautiful finish on the outside of the structure. The overall height of the tank is 137 feet 10 inches. The tank proper is a true ellipse and is 46 feet in diameter and 32 feet 6 inches high at the center. The range in head from high and low water lines is 26 feet.

The three supporting columns are 5-1/2 feet in diameter. One contains the inlet-outlet piping, overflow, heater piping, and a ladder which furnishes access to the inside of the tank as well as to the top of the structure. Three sets of struts in the lower portion of the tower were used to reduce bending stresses in the columns due to wind loads.

The stainless-clad material required unusual and careful handling during fabrication, shipping and erection to keep the stainless surface from being damaged. The prime requirement was to keep the highly polished exterior surface perfectly preserved without highlights or variations. Experiments prior to starting the work on the material proved it was impossible to satisfactorily re-polish areas which were scratched or otherwise marred.

The plates were inspected at the mill (in Plainfield, Illinois) to be sure they had a good, uniform polish. Before shipment from the mill, the stainless surface was protected by a sprayed application of plastic, which after hardening was covered with a heavy paper applied with an adhesive.

Upon arrival at our Birmingham plant, the handling was held to a minimum and each plate was moved into the fabrication area only as needed. All hooks and slings used to handle the material were protected with a rubber material.

The protective covering was never removed during fabrication, shipping or erection except along the seams and at locations where erection devices, lifting lugs, etc., were to be welded.

If heated by welding or burning on the carbon steel side of the plate or in a seam the plastic and masking tape produced a discoloration on the stainless clad surface that was impossible to remove. It was therefore necessary to strip back approximately six inches of the coating from any area that was to be welded or burned.

After welding or burning was completed, the slight discoloration caused by heating was removed by an electrolytic process using "electric swab" phosphoric acid. The areas were then rubbed and polished, after which the coating of plastic and paper was replaced. Extreme care was taken to protect the polished surface next to the welded seams from weld spatters and scratching.

All erection work on the outside of the tower and underneath the bottom was done from a tubular scaffold erected from ground level. Outside work on the top half of the tank was performed from a rolling scaffold, the upper end of which was attached to the derrick supporting the tower used for erection. The lower end was equipped with rubber tired wheels which rolled around the tank as erection progressed.

The final operation in the erection of the structure consisted of removing the masking tape and the plastic coating after which the highly-polished surface was cleaned with soft cloths. As a result of the extreme care taken in the shop and field, there are no visible defects on the outside surface of the structure.

The tank was erected by Foremen R. R. Boatman and Carl Dewyer and their crew. Saarinen & Associates, Detroit, architects for the Technical Center, conceived the shape and appearance for the tank.

The completed structure furnishes a striking example of cooperation between the final owner, architect and constructors to produce a functional design utilizing special materials and surface treatment to harmonize with the modern automotive industry.

"The Water Tower," folder 230, box 102, Eero Saarinen Collection, MS 593, Series IV, Yale University Archives

opposite
Technical Center water tower,
ca. 1952

Press clips about the General Motors Technical Center

What General Motors needed was a dignified headquarters for research performed by its various independent and autonomous branches. As the problem was developed, it became more and more evident to the architects…that the basic need was for radical flexibility and provision for expansion.…The great trick would be to keep the effect of finish at every stage; the child, though he is not yet a man, must be a complete child.…

To implement their new ideal of radical expandability held in constant balance, the architects began by creating uniform and interchangeable standards wherever possible.…Contrary to common opinion, these big uniformities, far from producing monotony, will tend instead to give full value to every change of pace and change of shape as the visitor threads his car through the wooded, lake-shore compound.

The General Motors Technical Center will serve as a standing refutation to those who conceive so highly industrialized an operation as being in its nature "purely mechanical" and "anti-human." In all essentials it depends on qualities of perception, of insight, of human spirit.

"G. M. Technical Center," *Architectural Forum*, July 1949, 70–78

What did Saarinen accomplish in giving final shape to all this industrial effort? He did the appropriate thing…he blazed an industrial trail into the no-man's-land of architecture which today lies between modern romanticism and the new classicism. He accomplished this by concentrating on two things: 1) Making the building work mechanically by integrating the disciplines of such matters as air conditioning and lighting with the classic pure shapes and expressive proportions of the structure. 2) Retaining the romantic heritage by using vivid hues and special glazes not seen since the heyday of the Persians. "If a large building today must be impersonal," he seems to have said, "let it at least have an exciting impersonality."

"General Motors Technical Center," *Architectural Forum*, November 1951, 111–23

The achievement, which is Saarinen's, is to have held all this advanced technology under admirable control in designing an integrated series of buildings that are modern but not freakish, functional but not barren, imposing but not overblown, clean and cool in line but with an underlying warmth achieved through a bold orchestration and notable architectural use of color.

"G.M. Technical Center," *Fortune*, December 1951, 82–86

Mr. Saarinen once said that "the architect's job is to make a proud order out of the form-world of our industrial era." Here he has done just that, and has produced a masterpiece.…

An infinite number of a few types of mass-produced identical parts gives a regularity which might do more than assure unity: it might congeal into monotony. From this the design is rescued by adroitly introduced variations and surprises.…

There are bold variations in color, particularly successful in the rectangular brick walls prominently forming the ends of so many of the buildings.…The unabashed sensuousness of the color and its welcoming of natural variations in tone and surface make a vivid and appropriate contrast to the precise "machine-age" aesthetic of the repeated mass-produced elements.…

The whole Center has the quality of a machine-made product, but it manages…to be a product which is a wonderfully gratifying work of art.…While our machine-made vocabulary cannot convey everything, it can, and here does, express certain kinds of essentially contemporary emotional content which no past forms could ever convey with such force and meaning. Whatever does this is major architecture.

John McAndrews, "General Motors Technical Center," *Art in America*, Spring 1956, 26–33

It is a truly American melding of the best from Europe, with native American feeling: a much-needed demonstration that these sources can be improved for our consumption.…To my mind it is a milestone of the stature of the Barcelona Pavilion and a healthy use of Mies' influence too rarely seen.

John Dinwiddie, in "One Hundred Years of Significant Building," *Architectural Record*, July 1956

Are the interiors handsome, do they work? You bet. And sometimes they're knock-outs, too. Then where are our superlatives; why equivocate? Because bright and shiny talent and money have only harvested a glorified product from a well-plowed field.... Grand as the scale may be, GM's Styling staff is still straddling two worlds. Ingenious electric devices are embedded in a lovingly hand-crafted cherry desk, spare and shiny chromed furniture stands on handloomed wool rugs, and a standard-issue receptionist rises from a fiber glass bowl in the lobby. In taking what they deem, possibly, the best of two worlds, GM's Styling organization has demonstrated that it is no more and no less than anyone else still seeking a course. GM President Harlow H. Curtice has said, "There are no 'todays' at the Technical Center. This is our investment in tomorrows." Perhaps. There are nevertheless, plenty "yesterdays" on the premises.

"What's Good Enough for General Motors," *Interiors*, January 1957

In the course of the General Motors job, Eero learned to smoke cigars, but he learned a great deal more besides. He had already a practical instinct for problem-solving methods of a kind which in a formal version would be called operations research. He had an intuitive grasp of the branching structure of alternative strategies; if instinct or evidence suggested, he wouldn't hesitate to go back down the tree and start along another route—keeping the effort invested up to that point only as background and experience....

By the time the center was completed, Eero had become a master of the feedback principle.... In the work that followed, Eero intensified his pursuit of the concept and the structure peculiarly appropriate to each particular problem. It is this consistent attitude that gives continuity to Eero's architecture; each building is in effect a model of the particular problem it seeks to answer.

Charles Eames, "General Motors Revisited: A Special Report by Charles Eames," *Architectural Forum*, June 1971, 21–28

NOTES

Preface

1 For more on this topic, see Jayne Merkel, *Eero Saarinen* (New York: Phaidon, 2005), 75.

Chapter One

1 Lawrence Gustin, *Billy Durant, Creator of General Motors* (Flushing, MI: Craneshaw, 1984), 49, 47.

2 Gustin, *Billy Durant*, 15. Flint, Michigan, was home to the Durant-Dort Carriage Company. It was known as the "Vehicle City" for its production of more than one hundred thousand carriages, buggies, and carts each year.

3 Ibid., 69, 87.

4 William Pelfrey, *General Motors, Priorities and Focus: Yesterday, Today and Tomorrow* (Detroit: General Motors University, 2000), 16.

5 Gustin, *Billy Durant*, 140–42.

6 Pelfrey, *General Motors, Priorities and Focus*, 17.

7 Gustin, *Billy Durant*, 157.

8 Pelfrey, *General Motors, Priorities and Focus*, 17.

9 Ibid., 18.

10 Arthur Pound, *The Turning Wheel: The Story of General Motors through Twenty-Five Years 1908–1933* (Garden City, NY: Doubleday, 1934), 380–94.

11 Pound, *Turning Wheel*, 168–69.

12 Pelfrey, *General Motors, Priorities and Focus*, 19.

13 Gustin, *Billy Durant*, 204–18, 248–61.

14 Pound, *Turning Wheel*, 193–208.

15 Alfred P. Sloan Jr., "General Motors Corporation Organization Study," 1920, 2, General Motors Business Library Collection, General Motors Heritage Center, Sterling Heights, MI. See also Donaldson Brown, "Decentralized Operations and Responsibilities with Coordinated Control in General Motors," February 1927, General Collection, General Motors Heritage Center.

16 Alfred P. Sloan Jr., *My Years with General Motors* (New York: Currency Doubleday, 1963/1990), 165–68, 238–47.

17 Ibid., 149–68.

18 *Sixteenth Annual Report of General Motors Corporation, Year Ended December 31, 1924*, General Collection, General Motors Heritage Center, 8.

19 Kettering Archives, General Motors Research Library, ca. 1964, General Collection, General Motors Heritage Center, 4.

20 See, respectively, Charles Franklin Kettering public relations biography, March 1955, 5, DN363, General Motors Executive Biographies Collection, General Motors Heritage Center; Lerinda Frost, *General Motors Research and Development Center: 75 Years of Inspiration, Imagination and Innovation* (Detroit: General Motors Corporation, 1995), 14; *General Motors Research and Development Center*, 17; Kettering public relations biography, 8, 27.

21 T. A. Boyd, *Professional Amateur: The Biography of Charles Franklin Kettering* (New York: E. P. Dutton, 1957), 141.

22 Stephen Bayley, *Harley Earl* (New York: Taplinger, 1990), 23.

23 George Moon, *An American Versailles, Eero Saarinen and the General Motors Technical Center: A Privilege Remembered*, author copy, unpublished manuscript, n.d., 54. See also Bayley, *Harley Earl*, 26.

24 Michael Lamm and Dave Holls, *A Century of Automotive Style: 100 Years of American Car Design* (Stockton, CA: Lamm-Morada, 1997), 85; Bayley, *Harley Earl*, 30.

25 Bayley, *Harley Earl*, 26.

26 Ibid., 32–33.

27 Lamm and Holls, *A Century of Automotive Style*, 87; see also Maurice D. Hendry, *Cadillac: Standard of the World, The Complete History* (Kutztown, PA: Automobile Quarterly, 1996), 435.

28 David Temple, *The Cars of Harley Earl* (Forest Lake, MN: CarTech, 2016), 13.

29 Harley Earl also designed a custom Pierce-Arrow, rebodied by Don Lee, in 1920 for Fatty Arbuckle that was similarly influenced by the Hispano-Suiza. Details such as the grille shape and hood louvers of later Cadillacs of the 1930s likewise recalled the Hispanos. Lamm and Holls, *A Century of Automotive Style*, 87.

30 Bayley, *Harley Earl*, 46; Ron Van Gelderen and Matt Larson, *LaSalle: Cadillac's Companion Car* (Paducah, KY: Turner, 2000), 9.

31 The 1928 LaSalle sales brochures lists sixteen standard body types and two Fleetwood Special Custom body types.

32 Lamm and Holls, *A Century of Automotive Style*, 89. "Dozens of automakers already had one or two person styling staffs." Lamm and Holls, *A Century of Automotive Style*, 72.

33 Bayley, *Harley Earl*, 47.

34 Sloan, *My Years with General Motors*, 269.

35 Bayley, *Harley Earl*, 42–43.

36 Stanley H. Brams, *The Skillful Men* (self-published, 1954), 2.

37 Brams, *Skillful Men*, 1; Bayley, *Harley Earl*, 48.

38 William L. Mitchell public relations biography, October 1972, General Collection, General Motors Heritage Center.

39 At the time that individual studios were established by the GM Styling section, GM had, for the most part, scaled its passenger car and truck offerings to its classic lineup: Buick, Cadillac, Chevrolet, GMC, Oldsmobile, and Pontiac. The Cadillac studio would continue to design the LaSalle until 1940. All other earlier brands had ceased to exist, including the Oakland, which had been replaced in favor of its companion, Pontiac, after the 1932 model year.

40 Bayley, *Harley Earl*, 45.

41 Lamm and Holls, *A Century of Automotive Style*, 102, 103.

42 Bayley, *Harley Earl*, 57.

43 Karl Ludvigsen, "Retrospect: 1938 Buick 'Y' Show Car," *MotorTrend*, March 1974, 61; press release, *Buick News*, GM Public Relations, July 30, 1990, General Collection, General Motors Heritage Center.

44 Lamm and Holls, *A Century of Automotive Style*, 88–89.

45 Other protégés included Eugene Bordinat, who led design for Ford Motor Company from 1961 to 1980; Elwood Engel, who helmed design at Chrysler from 1961 to 1974; and Richard Teague, who was vice president of design at American Motors from 1964 to 1983. Lamm and Holls, *A Century of Automotive Style*, 106.

46 See Carroll Gantz, *Design Chronicles: Significant Mass-Produced Designs of the 20th Century* (Atglen, PA: Schiffer, 2005), 125; Leon Whiteson, "Art Center: The Postwar Years," *Review* 3, no. 2 (July 1991): 12; Thomas Lockwood, *Design Thinking: Integrating Innovation, Customer Experience, and Brand Value* (New York: Allworth, 2009), 7.

47 General Motors News Release, September 3, 1940, General Collection, General Motors Heritage Center.

48 William Pelfrey, *Billy, Alfred and General Motors: The Story of Two Unique Men, a Legendary Company, and a Remarkable Time in American History* (New York: AMACOM, 2006), 270.

49 David Farber, *Sloan Rules: Alfred P. Sloan and the Triumph of General Motors* (Chicago: University of Chicago Press, 2002), 220.

50 Allen Orth, "The War Years," September 18, 1956, General Motors Business Library Collection, General Motors Heritage Center, 18.

51 Sloan, *My Years with General Motors*, 386.

52 General Motors News Release, June 12, 1940, General Collection, General Motors Heritage Center.

53 *37th Annual Report of General Motors Corporation for the Year Ended December 31, 1945*, 28, General Collection, General Motors Heritage Center. Total war production for all General Motors US plants during World War II, as noted in the 1945 annual report, included the following: 119,562,000 shells; 39,181,000 cartridge cases; 206,000 airplane engines, including jet propulsion engines; 13,000 complete bomber and fighter planes; 97,000 aircraft propellers; 301,000 aircraft gyroscopes; 38,000 tanks, tank destroyers, and armored vehicles; 854,000 trucks, including amphibious ducks (DUKWs); 190,000 cannons; 1,900,000 machine guns and submachine guns; 3,142,000 carbines; 3,826,000 electric motors of all kinds; 11,111,000 fuzes [sic]; 360,000,000 ball and roller bearings; 198,000 diesel engines for army and navy use; and many other products.

54 Sloan, *My Years with General Motors*, 382.

55 A. P. Sloan to C. F. Kettering, "Research Laboratories Division—Trend of Policy," March 29, 1944, General Collection, General Motors Heritage Center, 1, 3.

56 E. V. Rippingille to C. F. Kettering, April 11, 1944, 3–4, General Collection, General Motors Heritage Center.

Chapter Two

1 *37th Annual Report of General Motors Corporation for the Year Ended December 31, 1945*, General Collection, General Motors Heritage Center, 28, 14, 15.

2 Alfred P. Sloan Jr., *My Years with General Motors* (New York: Currency Doubleday, 1963/1990), 259.

3 Ibid., 261.

4 Ibid., 262.

5 "A History of the Development and Construction of the General Motors Technical Center," Warren Township, Macomb County, Michigan, July 30, 1954, General Collection, General Motors Heritage Center, 1.

6 General Motors Office of the Secretary, minutes of the GM Administration Committee, December 13, 1944, General Collection, General Motors Heritage Center. The Administration Committee was established by senior executive leadership in 1937 to administer and execute high-level policies created by the Policy Committee. It was composed entirely of corporate operating officers. Members in 1944 included Albert Bradley, who succeeded Sloan as board chair, serving from 1956 to 1958; Frederic Donner, who served from 1958 to 1967; and Harlow H. "Red" Curtice, who served as president of General Motors during the postwar boom years of 1953 to 1958.

7 Ibid.

8 George Moon, *An American Versailles, Eero Saarinen and the General Motors Technical Center: A Privilege Remembered*, author copy, unpublished manuscript, n.d., 77.

9 "Albert Kahn, Inducted 2012," Automotive Hall of Fame, October 22, 2018, http://www.automotivehalloffame.org/honoree/albert-kahn/. Ethyl Corporation was a joint venture of General Motors and Standard Oil. It manufactured the antiknock fuel additive tetraethyl lead (TEL), which was pioneered by Kettering's GM Research laboratories.

10 Moon, *American Versailles*, 141. See also New York World's Fair 1939–1940 Records, New York Public Library.

11 Sloan, *My Years with General Motors*, 262.

12 LeRoy E. Kiefer personnel file, box 4, folder 17, Design Personnel Files, GM Design Archive & Special Collections, General Motors, Warren, MI. There's no existing record of why the Saarinens were recommended, although Eliel's design of Cranbrook had established his national reputation as a modernist architect and his idealized goals for architecture aligned with the overall vision of GM's

management. In 1943 he had published a master plan in *The City* that included the city of Warren. In this early example of postwar rationalist planning, Saarinen had presented a design research methodology similar to that used in industrial science to reach conclusions based on assessment of experimental data. It's possible that GM executives were aware of this document.

13 Moon, *American Versailles*, 163.

14 Ibid., 161, 76–77.

15 C. F. Huddle in discussion with T. A. Boyd, Oral History Project, Kettering Archives, General Motors Research Library, November 10, 1964.

16 Quoted in Sloan, *My Years with General Motors*, 263.

17 Ibid.

18 Moon, *American Versailles*, 99.

19 "Architect Selected for GMC Technical Center," *Michigan Contractor and Builder* 39, no. 15 (July 28, 1945): 1, Swanson Family Papers, Cranbrook Archive, Bloomfield Hills, MI.

20 Albert Christ-Janer, *Eliel Saarinen, Finnish-American Architect and Educator* (Chicago and London: University of Chicago Press, 1979), xvii.

21 Marika Hausen, Kirmo Mikkola, Anna-Lisa Amberg, and Tytti Valto, *Eliel Saarinen, Projects 1896–1923* (Cambridge: MIT Press, 1990), 10.

22 See "Finland, the Big Little Country of Architecture," *Suomi Finland*, December 19, 2016, https://toolbox.finland.fi/presentations/arts-culture/finland-the-little-big-country-of-architecture/.

23 Robert R. McCormick, quoted in "The International Competition for a New Administration Building for the *Chicago Tribune* MCMXXII: containing all the designs submitted in response to the *Chicago Tribune*'s Offer Commemorating Its Seventy-Fifth Anniversary, June 10, 1922" (Tribune Company, 1923).

24 Katherine Solomonson, *The Chicago Tribune Tower Competition: Skyscraper Design and Cultural Change in the 1920s* (Chicago and London: University of Chicago Press, 2003), 1, 171.

25 Willard Connely, *Louis Sullivan as He Lived, the Shaping of American Architecture: A Biography* (New York: Horizon, 1960), 291.

26 Eeva-Liisa Pelkonen and Donald Albrecht, eds., *Eero Saarinen: Shaping the Future* (New Haven: Yale University Press, 2006), 324.

27 Hausen et al., *Eliel Saarinen, Projects 1896–1923*, 38.

28 Pelkonen and Albrecht, *Eero Saarinen*, 324.

29 Marianne Strengell, interview by Robert Brown, January 8–December 16, 1982, Archives of American Art, Smithsonian Institution, https://www.aaa.si.edu/collections/interviews/oral-history-interview-marianne-strengell-12411, 8.

30 Mark Coir, "Cranbrook: A Brief History," Cranbrook Educational Community, 2005, http://www.cranbrook.edu/sites/default/files/ftpimages/120/misc/misc_47669.pdf, 3.

31 Ibid., 5.

32 Strengell, interview by Robert Brown, 32.

33 David G. De Long, "Eliel Saarinen and the Cranbrook Tradition in Architecture and Urban Design," in *Design in America, The Cranbrook Vision 1925–1950* (New York: Harry N. Abrams, 1984), 61–62.

34 Ruth Adler Schnee, oral history, January 16, 2009, GM Design Archive & Special Collections, General Motors.

35 "Development and Construction," 2.

36 General Motors Office of the Secretary, minutes of the GM Board of Directors, May 7, 1945, General Collection, General Motors Heritage Center.

37 General Motors News Release, July 24, 1945, General Collection, General Motors Heritage Center.

38 Moon, *American Versailles*, 102, 177.

39 "G.M. Technical Center," *Architectural Forum*, July 1949, 71.

40 General Motors, "To Speed the Pace of Progress," advertisement, *Life*, September 24, 1945, 54–55.

41 Nancy Ann Miller, "Eero Saarinen on the Frontier of the Future: Building Corporate Image in the American Suburban Landscape, 1939–1961" (PhD diss., University of Pennsylvania, 1999), 21–22.

42 Louise A. Mozingo, *Pastoral Capitalism: A History of Suburban Corporate Landscapes* (Cambridge: MIT Press, 2011), 74–75.

43 "General Motors Technical Center to Unite Science with Its Application," *Architectural Record*, November 1945, 98–103.

44 *37th Annual Report of General Motors Corporation*, 25, 24.

45 Eliel Saarinen to W. J. Davidson, GM Corporation, September 2, 1948, Kevin Roche Collection, GM Design Archive & Special Collections, General Motors.

46 For a further description of the site, see Buffalo Public and Grosvenor Libraries Press Release, n.d., folder 18, box 1, series I, Tech Center Research Collection, General Motors Design Archive & Special Collections.

47 Moon, *American Versailles*, 100.

48 Photographs of model, folder 278, box 138, series IV, Eero Saarinen Collection, Yale University Archives.

49 Reinhold Martin, *The Organizational Complex: Architecture, Media, and Corporate Space* (Cambridge: MIT Press, 2003), 129.

50 Moon, *American Versailles*, 100.

51 "Development and Construction," 2.

52 Site preparation blueprint set, Facilities Department, General Motors Technical Center, Warren, Michigan; "Development and Construction," 2.

53 General Motors News Release, October 25, 1945, General Collection, General Motors Heritage Center.

54 Clipping from unidentified newspaper, August 1945, folder 1, box 3, J. Robert Swanson and Pipsan Saarinen Swanson Papers, Cranbrook Archives; "Development and Construction," 2–3.

55 Mina Marefat, "Washington DC, USA—Revealed: Eero Saarinen's Secret Wartime Role in the White House," *Architectural Review*, October 25, 2010, http://www.architectural-review.com/view/washinton-dc-usa-revealed-eero-saarinens-secret-wartime-role-in-the-white-house/8607195.article; Wendy Gilmartin, "The Secret Life of Eero Saarinen, Architect of the St. Louis Arch and…the White House War Room?," *L.A. Weekly*, October 9, 2012, http://www.laweekly.com/arts/the-secret-life-of-eero-saarinen-architect-of-the-st-louis-arch-andthe-white-house-war-room-2371000.

56 National Register of Historic Places registration form, General Motors Technical Center, National Park Service, United States Department of the Interior, 2000, 41.

57 Walter P. Reuther, UAW-CIO, to Charles E. Wilson, General Motors Corporation, August 18, 1945, as found in General Motors Strike Historical Documents, volume 1, 1945–1946, 2, General Motors Heritage Center.

58 Ibid., 5.

59 Walter W. Ruch, "180,000 Quit Jobs," *New York Times*, November 22, 1945, as found in General Motors Strike Historical Documents, volume 1, 1945–1946, General Collection, General Motors Heritage Center.

60 Louis Stark, "Truman Names Fact Finders for GM, Defying Opposition; Labor Curb Passed by House," *New York Times*, December 12, 1945, as found in General Motors Strike Historical Documents, volume 2, 1945–1946, General Collection, General Motors Heritage Center.

61 "Anderson Announces Terms of GM-UAW Settlement to Press," March 13, 1946, radio reports, transcript, special for General Motors Corporation, as found in General Motors Strike Historical Documents, volume 2, 1945–1946, General Collection, General Motors Heritage Center.

62 Sloan, *My Years with General Motors*, 263.

63 $100 million in 1946 is equivalent to $1.3 billion in 2019 dollars.

64 General Motors Administration Committee, meeting minutes, March 1, 1946, GM Office of the Secretary. The Chevrolet Light Car program was a project to create an all-new lightweight and more economical car for the US market as well as manufacturing facilities outside Cleveland, Ohio, to build it. It was announced to the public on May 15, 1945. GM announced its indefinite deferral in September 1946, citing shortages in materials, even though product development continued internally, as evidenced by the showing of a Light Car prototype at a meeting of the executive leadership at the GM Proving Ground in Milford, Michigan, in April 1947.

65 "Development and Construction," 3, 6.

Chapter Three

1 General Motors Office of the Secretary, minutes of the GM Administration Committee, July 29, 1948.

2 Joseph Lacy, "Memoirs of Joseph N. Lacy," unpublished manuscript, n.d., Cranbrook Archives, 9.

3 Mark Coir, "The Cranbrook Factor," in *Eero Saarinen, Shaping the Future*, ed. Eeva-Liisa Pelkonen and Donald Albrecht (New Haven: Yale University Press, 2006), 39.

4 George Moon, *An American Versailles, Eero Saarinen and the General Motors Technical Center: A Privilege Remembered*, author copy, unpublished manuscript, n.d., 116.

5 Charles Eames, "General Motors Revisited," *Architectural Forum* 134, no. 5 (June 1971): 21–28.

6 *New York Times* interview, January 29, 1953, quoted in Eero Saarinen, *Eero Saarinen on His Work: A Selection of Buildings Dating from 1947 to 1964 with Statements by the Architect*, ed. Aline B. Saarinen (New Haven and London: Yale University Press, 1962), 14.

7 John L. Dorman, "Eero Saarinen's Michigan," *New York Times*, October 6, 2017, https://www.nytimes.com/2017/10/06/travel/eero-saarinen-michigan-architecture-modernist-design.html.

8 Coir, "Cranbrook Factor," 30.

9 Jari Jetsonen and Sirkkaliisa Jetsonen, *Saarinen Houses* (New York: Princeton Architectural Press, 2014), 11.

10 Coir, "Cranbrook Factor," 32.

11 Eliel Saarinen documentary feature project, directed by Eric Saarinen (Harbor City, CA: Eric Saarinen Films, 2017), DVD.

12 Paul Goldberger, "The Cranbrook Vision," *New York Times Magazine*, April 8, 1984, 51.

13 Cranbrook Academy of Art catalog, October 1932, Cranbrook Academy of Art Publications, 1998-05e, Series V: Catalogs, 1936–1948, Cranbrook Archives, Cranbrook Academy of Art.

14 Lilian Swann Saarinen, interview by Robert Brown, 1979–81, Cambridge, Massachusetts, Archives of American Art, Smithsonian Institution.

15 Lacy, "Memoirs," 19–20.

16 Lilian Swann Saarinen, interview by Robert Brown.

17 National Register of Historic Places registration form, General Motors Technical Center, National Park Service, United States Department of the Interior, January 19, 2000, 41.

18 Coir, "Cranbrook Factor," 37.

19 "A History of the Development and Construction of the General Motors Technical Center," Warren Township, Macomb County, Michigan, July 30, 1954, General Collection, General Motors Heritage Center, 4.

20 Lacy, "Memoirs," 13.

21 Brian Carter and Balthazar Korab, *Between Earth and Sky* (Ann Arbor: University of Michigan, A. Alfred Taubman College of Architecture + Urban Planning, 2003), 8.

22 Eames, "General Motors Revisited," 23; Lacy, "Memoirs," 21.

23 "Development and Construction," 9.

24 Letter from Eero Saarinen to Astrid Sampe, 1948, Astrid Sampe Papers, #1995–87, Cranbrook Archives.

25 Joseph N. Lacy, Saarinen, Saarinen and Associates, to Mr. W. J. Davidson, General Motors Corporation, February 14, 1949, Kevin Roche Collection, GM Design Archive & Special Collections, General Motors.

26 Carter and Korab, *Between Earth and Sky*, 9.

27 Edward Eichstedt, "Current Work in Progress," *Landscape Architecture* 42, no. 4 (July 1952): 167.

28 Ibid., 10.

29 "G.M. Technical Center," *Architectural Forum* 91, no. 1 (July 1949): 71.

30 Lacy, "Memoirs," 22.

31 Kevin Roche oral history, March 8, 2018, GM Design Archive & Special Collections, General Motors.

32 Lacy, "Memoirs," 15.

33 "Development and Construction," 4.

34 Eero Saarinen & Associates to Smith, Hinchman & Grylls, Inc., December 29, 1950, Kevin Roche Collection, GM Design Archive & Special Collections, General Motors.

35 National Register of Historic Places registration form, 43.

36 Kevin Roche oral history.

37 Lacy, "Memoirs," 21.

38 Moon, *American Versailles*, 177.

39 Coir, "Cranbrook Factor," 234.

40 Pierluigi Serraino, "Modelmaking Rangers: Form-Makers in Action at Eero Saarinen and Associates," in *Solid States: Concrete in Transition*, ed. Michael Bell and Craig Buckley (New York: Princeton Architectural Press, 2010), 47.

41 Eames, "General Motors Revisited," 24.

42 "Caldwell Air Conditioning Controversial New System Uses Many Special Devices to Get Hurricane Speeds and Kinetic Energy Diffusion," *Architectural Forum* 93, no. 1 (July 1950): 114–17.

43 Coir, "Cranbrook Factor," 233.

44 "General Motors Technical Center," *Architectural Forum* 95, no. 5 (November 1951): 112.

45 Kevin Roche oral history.

46 Ibid.; Ruth Adler Schnee oral history, January 16, 2009, GM Design Archive & Special Collections, General Motors.

47 National Register of Historic Places registration form, 5.

48 Ibid.

49 Eichstedt, "Current Work in Progress," 166.

50 National Register of Historic Places registration form, 5.

51 Eero Saarinen, "The Challenge to the Arts Today," in *Seventy-Five* (New Haven: Yale University Press, 1953), 113, 191. See also "The Maturing Modern," *Time*, July 2, 1956, 57; Donald Albrecht, "The Clients and Their Architect," in *Eero Saarinen: Shaping the Future*, ed. Eeva-Liisa Pelkonen and Donald Albrecht (New Haven: Yale University Press, 2006), 46.

52 "Technical Center History," press kit package, General Motors Public Relations, 1956, folder 253, box 136, series IV, Yale University Archives.

Chapter Four

1 General Motors News Release, May 22, 1949, General Collection, General Motors Heritage Center.

2 Joseph Lacy, "Memoirs of Joseph N. Lacy," unpublished manuscript, Cranbrook Archives, n.d., p. 14.

3 Thomas J. Holleman and James P. Gallagher, *Smith, Hinchman & Grylls, 125 Years of Architecture and Engineering, 1853–1978* (Detroit: Wayne State University Press, 1978), 147–48.

4 "A History of the Development and Construction of the General Motors Technical Center," Warren Township, Macomb County, Michigan, July 30, 1954, General Collection, General Motors Heritage Center, 6. See also General Motors News Release, July 11, 1949, General Collection, General Motors Heritage Center.

5 "Development and Construction," 6–7.

6 "Architectural Notes on Research Staff Building at the General Motors Technical Center," General Collection, General Motors Heritage Center, 1.

7 "Architectural Notes on Engineering Staff Building at the General Motors Technical Center," General Collection, General Motors Heritage Center.

8 "Architectural Notes on Process Development Section of General Motors Technical Center," General Collection, General Motors Heritage Center.

9 Joseph H. Karshner, "Technical Center Shorts," in *GM Technical Center History*, 1955, General Collection, General Motors Heritage Center, 4.

10 "Architectural Notes on the Styling Section of the General Motors Technical Center," General Collection, General Motors Heritage Center.

11 "Architectural Notes on the Service Section of the General Motors Technical Center" and "Architectural Notes on the Central Restaurant Building of the General Motors Technical Center," both in General Collection, General Motors Heritage Center.

12 Eero Saarinen, *Eero Saarinen on His Work: A Selection of Buildings Dating from 1947 to 1964 with Statements by the Architect*, ed. Aline B. Saarinen (New Haven and London: Yale University Press, 1962), 28.

13 Edward A. Eichstedt, "Current Work in Progress: Landscape at the General Motors Technical Center," *Landscape Architecture* 42, no. 4 (July 1952): 166.

14 Ibid., 166–67.

15 Joseph H. Karshner, *General Motors Technical Center Architectural Summary*, April 1966, General Collection, General Motors Heritage Center.

16 Saarinen, *Eero Saarinen on His Work*, 24.

17 Ibid.

18 "Building Engineering," *Architectural Forum* 102, no. 4 (April 1955): 163.

19 George Moon, *An American Versailles, Eero Saarinen and the General Motors Technical Center: A Privilege Remembered*, author copy, unpublished manuscript, n.d., 364.

20 Ibid., 358.

21 "Development and Construction," 11.

22 Lacy, "Memoirs," 13.

23 Kevin Roche, oral history, March 8, 2018, GM Design Archive & Special Collections, General Motors.

24 "Development and Construction," 38.

25 William Jarratt interviewed by Wesley Janz, 1992, and Joseph Lacy, interview #1 by Wesley Janz, 1992, Wesley R. Janz, Cranbrook Archives.

26 "Development and Construction," 15; Moon, *American Versailles*, 350.

27 Lacy, "Memoirs," 13.

28 Eero Saarinen Papers, Approvals, folder 329, box 140, series IV, Yale Collection; "Development and Construction," 16.

29 United States v. Claycraft Company, 364 F. Supp. 1358 (S.D. Ohio 1972), https://law.justia.com/cases/federal/district-courts/FSupp/364/1358/2259330/.

30 Moon, *An American Versailles*, 346; Roche, oral history, March 8, 2018.

31 "Development and Construction," 17.

32 Eero Saarinen Papers, Approvals, folder 329, box 140, series IV, Yale Collection.

33 Moon, *American Versailles*, 298.

34 "Architectural Notes on the Styling Section," 6.

35 "Architectural Notes on the General Motors Technical Center Building Groups," General Collection, General Motors Heritage Center, 6.

36 "Development and Construction," 23, 29.

37 Harry Mitchell, "Gas Turbines to Be Tested in New, Modern Laboratory," *Lab Notes*, General Motors Research Laboratories Division, October 1953, General Collection, General Motors Heritage Center.

38 "Development and Construction," 31.

39 Kevin Roche, oral history, July 11, 2016, and March 8, 2018, GM Design Archive & Special Collections, General Motors.

40 Lacy, "Memoirs," 14.

41 "Development and Construction," 22.

42 Joseph H. Karshner, *GM Technical Center History*, complete first draft, 1955, General Collection, General Motors Heritage Center, 6.

Chapter Five

1 Russell Harris, "GM Technical Center Mirrors Bold Future," *Detroit News*, March 18, 1956, 16B.

2 *Ward's 1957 Automotive Yearbook* (Detroit: Ward's Reports, 1957), 148.

3 Kamal Khondkar, "100 Years-Dow Jones Industrial Average Chart History (updated)," TradingNInvestment, 2019, https://tradinginvestment.com/100-years-dow-jones-industrial-average-djia-events-history-chart/2/.

4 General Motors News Release, November 11, 1952, General Collection, General Motors Heritage Center.

5 Richard F. Weingroff, "Federal-Aid Highway Act of 1956: Creating the Interstate System," *Public Roads* 60, no. 1 (summer 1996), https://www.fhwa.dot.gov/publications/publicroads/96summer/p96su10.cfm.

6 "New York World's Fair Exhibit Voted Most Popular in Gallup Poll," *New York Times*, May 17, 1939, 19.

7 Eeva-Liisa Pelkonen and Donald Albrecht, eds., *Eero Saarinen: Shaping the Future* (New Haven: Yale University Press, 2006), 327.

8 Futurama narration, reprinted in Futurama souvenir book, issued in a limited edition of one thousand, "On the occasion of Paul Garrett's party at the University Club, 16 October 1939," box O/S 3, Bel Geddes Papers, Harry Ransom Center, University of Texas, Austin.

9 Kevin Roche, oral history, July 11, 2016, GM Design Archive & Special Collections, General Motors.

10 Donald Albrecht, "The Clients and Their Architect," in *Eero Saarinen: Shaping the Future*, 46.

11 General Motors Public Relations, *Where Today Meets Tomorrow: General Motors Technical Center* (Detroit: General Motors Corporation, 1956), General Collection, General Motors Heritage Center.

12 "At this new Technical Center we welcome the challenge of the future," General Motors advertisement, May–June 1956, DN680-1956-0160, General Motors Media Archive, General Motors.

13 "Pontiac Motorama Masterpieces" brochure, 1956, DASC.2017.009, GM Design Archive & Special Collections, General Motors.

14 *General Motors Engineering Journal* 3, no. 2 (1956); "Where Men Live in Tomorrow," *GM Folks* 19, no. 5 (May 1956): 12–16.

15 A. H. Raskin, "Key Men of Business," *New York Times Magazine*, May 13, 1956, 15.

16 George Moon, *An American Versailles, Eero Saarinen and the General Motors Technical Center: A Privilege Remembered*, author copy, unpublished manuscript, n.d., 403.

17 Ibid., 405.

18 Harlow H. Curtice, "Accelerating the Pace of Technological Progress," in *The Greatest Frontier: Remarks at the Dedication Program*, May 16, 1956, General Motors Technical Center, General Motors Public Relations Staff, General Collection, General Motors Heritage Center, 7.

19 Dr. Lawrence R. Hafstad, "The Future Is Our Assignment," in *Greatest Frontier*, 19–20.

20 Charles F. Kettering, "Let's Turn Around…and Look to the Future," in *Greatest Frontier*, 24.

21 Dwight Eisenhower, "The Rich Reward Ahead," in *Greatest Frontier*, 27.

22 Kevin Roche, oral histories, July 11, 2016, and March 8, 2018, GM Design Archive & Special Collections, General Motors.

23 Raymond Hayes, GM Department of Public Relations, General Motors Technical Center Dedication Correspondence, May 21, 1956, General Collection, General Motors Heritage Center.

24 *General Motors Technical Center Television Script: A Promise for America*, May 1, 1956, General Collection, General Motors Heritage Center, 1.

25 Moon, *American Versailles*, 412.

26 General Motors News Release, Wednesday, May 16, 1956, General Collection, General Motors Heritage Center, 1–3.

27 Moon, *American Versailles*, 407.

28 "General Motors Technical Center," *Fortune* (December 1951): 82.

29 "General Motors Technical Center," *Architectural Forum* 101, no. 5 (November 1954): 94–103.

30 W. Clifford Harvey, "An Industrial Disneyland," *Christian Science Monitor* (May 1956): 11.

31 "Where Tomorrows Are Born Today," *Detroit News Pictorial Magazine*, May 13, 1956, 20-21.

32 "One Hundred Years of Significant Buildings: Administration and Research Buildings," *Architectural Record* 119 (July 1956): 203.

33 Ibid., 204.

34 Ibid.

Chapter Six

1 "Architect Eero Saarinen," *Time*, July 2, 1956.

2 Ruth Adler Schnee to author, September 15, 2017.

3 Ruth Adler Schnee, oral history, January 16, 2009, GM Design Archive & Special Collections, General Motors.

4 Ibid.

5 Marion H. Bemis, "Marianne Strengell: Textile Consultant to Architect," *Handweaver & Craftsman* 8, no. 1 (winter 1956/1957): 6.

6 Ibid.

7 George Moon, *An American Versailles, Eero Saarinen and the General Motors Technical Center: A Privilege Remembered*, author copy, unpublished manuscript, n.d., 219.

8 Ibid., 221.

9 Agreements between GM and Eero Saarinen and Associates, folder 293, box 103, series IV, Eero Saarinen Collection, MS 593, Yale University Manuscripts and Archives.

10 Agreements between GM and Eero Saarinen and Associates, folder 235, box 103, series IV, Eero Saarinen Collection, MS 593, Yale University Manuscripts and Archives.

11 Alexander Girard to Joseph Lacy, April 21, 1955, folder 252, box 136, series IV, Eero Saarinen Collection, MS 593, Yale University Manuscripts and Archives.

12 Moon, *American Versailles*, 323.

13 "Interiors of the Styling Building in GM's Technical Center," *Contract Interiors* 116 (1957): 87.

14 Moon, *American Versailles*, 221.

15 Eero Saarinen, *Eero Saarinen on His Work: A Selection of Buildings Dating from 1947 to 1964 with Statements by the Architect*, ed. Aline B. Saarinen (New Haven and London: Yale University Press, 1962), 32.

16 Marc Treib, "Thomas Church (1902–1978)," in *Masters of Modern Landscape Design* (San Francisco: William Stout, 2003), 2.

17 Eero Saarinen, Dickinson College Arts Award Address, Carlisle, PA, December 1, 1959, folder 73, box 21, Eero Saarinen Papers, Yale University Manuscripts and Archives.

Chapter Seven

1 Eero Saarinen, *Eero Saarinen on His Work: A Selection of Buildings Dating from 1947 to 1964 with Statements by the Architect*, ed. Aline B. Saarinen (New Haven and London: Yale University Press, 1962), 24.

2 Ibid., 28.

3 George Moon, *An American Versailles, Eero Saarinen and the General Motors Technical Center: A Privilege Remembered*, author copy, unpublished manuscript, n.d., 298.

4 Ibid., 187.

5 Ibid., 161.

6 Ibid., 266.

7 Kevin Roche, oral history, July 11, 2016, GM Design Archive & Special Collections, General Motors.

8 Moon, *American Versailles*, 315.

9 Memorandum by Aline Saarinen to Eero Saarinen, August 9, 1954, and receipts, folder 264, box 137, series IV, Eero Saarinen Collection, MS 593, Yale University Manuscripts and Archives.

10 General Motors Public Relations, "Technical Center Shorts," General Motors Corporation, 1956, General Collection, General Motors Heritage Center, 1.

11 Harry Bertoia, tape-recorded interview by Paul Cummings, June 20, 1972, Archives of American Art, Smithsonian Institution.

12 Eero Saarinen to Mr. F. G. Tykle, General Motors Corporation, September 7, 1954, Kevin Roche Collection, GM Design Archive & Special Collections, General Motors.

13 Carlos Huber, "General Motors Technical Center," DoCoMoMo, February 24, 2007, http://www.drupal .docomomo-us.org/register/fiche/ general_motors_technical_center.

14 Charles Sheeler letter collection, 1939–58, Archives of American Art, Smithsonian Institution; correspondence between Daniel DiFabio and University of Michigan Museum of Art, January 29, 2001, folder 4, box 1, Research Art Files, GM Design Archive & Special Collections, General Motors.

15 Important Art Work in Styling, 1956, General Collection, General Motors Heritage Center.

16 Moon, *American Versailles*, 193, 235.

17 Ibid., 400.

18 "Architecture for the Future: GM Constructs a 'Versailles of Industry,'" *Life*, May 21, 1956, 102.

19 Mateo Kries and Jochen Eisenbrand, "List of Works, Buildings and Interiors: 1947–1949," *Alexander Girard: A Designer's Universe* (Weil am Rhein, Germany: Vitra Design Museum, 2016), 382.

20 "Architectural Notes on the General Motors Technical Center Building Groups," General Collection, General Motors Heritage Center, 4.

21 Kevin Roche, oral history, July 11, 2016.

Chapter Eight

1 Eero Saarinen, *Eero Saarinen on His Work: A Selection of Buildings Dating from 1947 to 1964 with Statements by the Architect*, ed. Aline B. Saarinen (New Haven and London: Yale University Press, 1962), 8.

2 Ibid.

3 "Summary of the Architecture of the General Motors Technical Center," General Collection, General Motors Heritage Center, 5.

4 Antonio Román, *Eero Saarinen: An Architecture of Multiplicity* (New York: Princeton Architectural Press, 2003), 28.

SELECTED BIBLIOGRAPHY

The primary and most important sources for this book came from the private archives of the General Motors Heritage Center, which houses an extensive collection of the company history, and the GM Design Archive & Special Collections (GMDASC), which is the official repository for the history of design. This consists of unpublished primary source materials such as letters, reports, business records, public relations documents, internal newsletters, transcripts, architectural drawings, sales brochures, oral histories, personnel files, meeting minutes, agreements, biographies, and advertisements. One of the most important is the unique unpublished memoir *An American Versailles* by George Moon, which provides an invaluable firsthand account of the project and the relationship between the Saarinen firm and General Motors.

The most profound visual resources were the GM Media Archive and the Madler Collection at the GMDASC. These collections house well over two hundred thousand photographic images documenting the history of the Technical Center.

I have also drawn heavily from the collections at Yale University Manuscripts and Archives, Cranbrook Archives, and Wayne State University Archives.

The bibliography that follows primarily lists published material.

Books

—

GM history

Farber, David. *Sloan Rules: Alfred P. Sloan and the Triumph of General Motors.* Chicago: University of Chicago Press, 2002.

Gustin, Lawrence. *Billy Durant, Creator of General Motors.* Flushing, MI: Craneshaw, 1984.

Pelfrey, William. *General Motors, Priorities and Focus: Yesterday, Today and Tomorrow.* Detroit: General Motors University, 2000.

———. *Billy, Alfred and General Motors: The Story of Two Unique Men, a Legendary Company, and a Remarkable Time in American History.* New York: AMACOM, 2006.

Pound, Arthur. *The Turning Wheel: The Story of General Motors through Twenty-Five Years 1908–1933.* Garden City, NY: Doubleday, 1934.

Sloan, Alfred P. Jr. *My Years with General Motors.* New York: Currency Doubleday, 1963/1990.

GM design history

Bayley, Stephen. *Harley Earl.* Paducah, KY: Turner, 2000.

Lamm, Michael, and Dave Holls. *A Century of Automotive Style: 100 Years of American Car Design.* Stockton, CA: Lamm-Morada, 1997.

General Motors Technical Center

Holleman, Thomas J., and James P. Gallagher. *Smith, Hinchman & Grylls, 125 Years of Architecture and Engineering, 1853–1978.* Detroit: Wayne State University Press, 1978.

Kries, Mateo, and Jochen Eisenbrand. *Alexander Girard: A Designer's Universe.* Weil am Rhein, Germany: Vitra Design Museum, 2016.

Mozingo Louise A. *Pastoral Capitalism: A History of Suburban Corporate Landscapes.* Cambridge: MIT Press, 2011.

Eliel and Eero Saarinen

Carter, Brian, and Balthazar Korab. *Between Earth and Sky.* Ann Arbor: University of Michigan, A. Alfred Taubman College of Architecture + Urban Planning, 2003.

Christ-Janer, Albert. *Eliel Saarinen, Finnish-American Architect and Educator.* Chicago and London: University of Chicago Press, 1979.

Hausen, Marika, Kirmo Mikkola, Anna-Lisa Amberg, and Tytti Valto. *Eliel Saarinen, Projects 1896–1923.* Cambridge: MIT Press, 1990.

Jetsonen, Jari, and Sirkkaliisa Jetsonen. *Saarinen Houses.* New York: Princeton Architectural Press, 2014.

Merkel, Jayne. *Eero Saarinen.* New York: Phaidon, 2005.

Pelkonen, Eeva-Liisa, and Donald Albrecht. *Eero Saarinen, Shaping the Future.* New Haven: Yale University Press, 2006.

Román, Antonio. *Eero Saarinen: An Architecture of Multiplicity.* New York: Princeton Architectural Press, 2003.

Saarinen, Aline B., ed. *Eero Saarinen on His Work: A Selection of Buildings Dating from 1947 to 1964 with Statements by the Architect.* New Haven and London: Yale University Press, 1962.

Saarinen, Eero. "The Challenge to the Arts Today." In *Seventy-Five.* New Haven: Yale University Press, 1953.

Serraino, Pierluigi. "Modelmaking Rangers: Form-Makers in Action at Eero Saarinen and Associates." In *Solid States: Concrete in Transition*, edited by Michael Bell and Craig Buckley, 47–60. New York: Princeton Architectural Press, 2010.

Periodicals

Architectural Forum. "Building Engineering." April 1955.

———. "Caldwell Air Conditioning Controversial New System Uses Many Special Devices to Get Hurricane Speeds and Kinetic Energy Diffusion." July 1950.

———. "General Motors Technical Center." November 1951.

———. "General Motors Technical Center." November 1954.

———. "G.M. Technical Center." July 1949.

Architectural Record. "General Motors Technical Center to Unite Science with Its Application." November 1945.

———. "One Hundred Years of Significant Buildings: Administration and Research Buildings." July 1956.

Bemis, Marion H. "Marianne Strengell: Textile Consultant to Architect." *Handweaver & Craftsman* 8, no. 1 (winter 1956/1957).

Clifford, Harvey W. "An Industrial Disneyland." *Christian Science Monitor.* May 1956.

Contract Interiors. "Interiors of the Styling Building in GM's Technical Center." 1957.

Detroit News Pictorial Magazine. "Where Tomorrows Are Born Today." May 13, 1956.

Eames, Charles. "General Motors Revisited." *Architectural Forum.* June 1971.

Eichstedt, Edward. "Current Work in Progress." *Landscape Architecture* 42, no. 4 (July 1952).

General Motors Engineering Journal 3, no. 2 (1956).

GM Folks. "Where Men Live in Tomorrow." May 1956.

Goldberger, Paul. "The Cranbrook Vision." *New York Times Magazine.* April 8, 1984.

Huber, Carlos. "General Motors Technical Center." *DoCoMoMo.* February 24, 2007.

Life. "Architecture for the Future: GM Constructs a 'Versailles of Industry.'" May 21, 1956.

Michigan Contractor and Builder. "Architect Selected for GMC Technical Center." Vol. 39, no. 15 (July 28, 1945).

Raskin, A. H. "Key Men of Business." *New York Times Magazine.* May 13, 1956.

Ruch, Walter W. "180,000 Quit Jobs." *New York Times.* November 22, 1945.

Time. "Architect Eero Saarinen." July 2, 1956.

Additional sources

General Motors. "To Speed the Pace of Progress." Advertisement in *Life.* September 24, 1945.

Miller, Nancy Ann. "Eero Saarinen on the Frontier of the Future: Building Corporate Image in the American Suburban Landscape, 1939–1961." PhD diss., University of Pennsylvania, 1999.

National Register of Historic Places registration form, General Motors Technical Center. National Park Service, United States Department of the Interior, 2000.

IMAGE CREDITS

Unless otherwise noted, all images are from
the collection of the General Motors Media Archive.

4–5, 6–7, 8–9: James Haefner
22 bottom: Collection of Kettering University Archives
27: From the Collections of the Henry Ford Foundation. Gift
    of the Family of William L. Mitchell
33: Walter Farynk
34: Max Habrecht, copyright Cranbrook Archives
38: Arcaid Images/Alamy Stock Photo
39: Richard G. Askew, copyright Cranbrook Archives
40: Atelier Apollo, 1922, courtesy Cranbrook Archives,
    Saarinen Family Papers
41 top left: Cranbrook Archives
41 bottom left: Harvey Croze, copyright Cranbrook Archives
41 right: Richard G. Askew, copyright Cranbrook Archives
43: Harvey Croze, copyright Cranbrook Archives
44 all: Rendering by Hugh Ferriss
45 top: General Motors Photographic Section, courtesy
    Cranbrook Archives
45 bottom: Rendering by Hugh Ferriss
50 bottom: Courtesy Walter P. Reuther Library
52: Courtesy Cranbrook Archives, Saarinen Family Papers
53: Copyright Cranbrook Archives
54 top: Courtesy Cranbrook Archives, Saarinen Family
    Papers
54 bottom: Copyright Cranbrook Archives
55 left: Max Habrecht, copyright Cranbrook Archives
55 right: Copyright Cranbrook Archives
56 all: Richard G. Askew, copyright Cranbrook Archives
57: Kevin Roche Collection DASC.2018.012, General Motors
    Design Archive & Special Collections
59 top: Courtesy Cranbrook Archives, Astrid Sampe
    Collection of Eero Saarinen Correspondence
60 top: Kevin Roche Collection DASC.2018.012, General
    Motors Design Archive & Special Collections
61 bottom, left and right: Richard Shirk, courtesy
    Cranbrook Archives
64: Copyright Cranbrook Archives, Claude de Forest
    Collection of Eero Saarinen and Associates Material
65 top and bottom: Richard Shirk, courtesy Cranbrook
    Archives
70 top: Eero Saarinen Collection (MS 593), Manuscripts and
    Archives, Yale University Library
70 center left, center right, and bottom: Richard Shirk,
    courtesy Cranbrook Archives
71 top: Eero Saarinen Collection (MS 593), Manuscripts and
    Archives, Yale University Library
72: Richard Knight, courtesy Kevin Roche
73: Eero Saarinen Collection (MS 593), Manuscripts and
    Archives, Yale University Library
83 right: Brad May
86 all: Eero Saarinen Collection (MS 593), Manuscripts and
    Archives, Yale University Library
87 top: Rodney Morr
87 bottom right: Tom Drew
92 bottom, left and right: Eero Saarinen Collection
    (MS 593), Manuscripts and Archives, Yale
    University Library
95 left: Susan Skarsgard
101 top: Copyright the *Detroit News*
108 bottom: Copyright Time/Life
110 all: Ezra Stoller
116 left: Scott Hyde, courtesy Cranbrook Archives, Florence
    Knoll Bassett Papers
117 all: Eero Saarinen Collection (MS 593), Manuscripts and
    Archives, Yale University Library
118 top: Carl Benkert Collection DASC.2017.012, General
    Motors Design Archive & Special Collections
119: Eero Saarinen Collection (MS 593), Manuscripts and
    Archives, Yale University Library

120: Carl Benkert Collection DASC.2017.012, General
    Motors Design Archive & Special Collections
122 top: Ezra Stoller
123: Courtesy Cranbrook Archives, S. Glen Paulsen Papers
128–29: Ezra Stoller
131: James Haefner
132–33: Balthazar Korab
134–35, 137: Ezra Stoller
138–39: Ezra Stoller, copyright Ezra Stoller/Esto
144–45, 148–49: James Haefner
150: Tom Drew
156: Lee Short
157: Tom Drew
158–59: James Haefner
160–61: Tom Drew
162–63: James Haefner
164: Ezra Stoller
165 top: Balthazar Korab, Library of Congress, Prints &
    Photographs Division, Balthazar Korab Archive at the
    Library of Congress, LC-DIG-krb-00069
165 bottom: Brad May
167 top right: Tom Drew
167 bottom: Balthazar Korab, Library of Congress, Prints &
    Photographs Division, Balthazar Korab Archive at the
    Library of Congress, LC-DIG-krb-00136
168, 170–71: Ezra Stoller
174–75: Balthazar Korab, Library of Congress, Prints &
    Photographs Division, Balthazar Korab Archive at the
    Library of Congress, LC-DIG-krb-00128
178 top: Ezra Stoller, copyright Ezra Stoller/Esto
178 bottom, 179: James Haefner
180–81: Carol M. Highsmith, Library of Congress, Prints &
    Photographs Division, Carol M. Highsmith, LC-DIG-
    highsm-13360
182–83: Tom Drew
184–85: James Haefner
191: Tom Drew
194–95: Ezra Stoller
198–99: Balthazar Korab, Library of Congress, Prints &
    Photographs Division, Balthazar Korab Archive at the
    Library of Congress, LC-DIG-krb-00113
202: Balthazar Korab, Library of Congress, Prints &
    Photographs Division, Balthazar Korab Archive at the
    Library of Congress, LC-DIG-krb-00075
203: Ezra Stoller
204–5: James Haefner
207: Balthazar Korab, Library of Congress, Prints &
    Photographs Division, Balthazar Korab Archive at the
    Library of Congress, LC-DIG-krb-00070
210 top: John Neuville
210 bottom right: James Haefner
211 top: Ezra Stoller
226 all: Tom Drew
232: Balthazar Korab, Library of Congress, Prints &
    Photographs Division, Balthazar Korab Archive at the
    Library of Congress, LC-DIG-krb-00049
234–35: James Haefner
238: Copyright *Detroit News*
243: Balthazar Korab, Library of Congress, Prints &
    Photographs Division, Balthazar Korab Archive at the
    Library of Congress, LC-DIG-krb-00069
256: Ezra Stoller

INDEX

This book is dedicated with respect
for the inventive and intelligent work
of this generous and kind being.

Kevin Roche
June 14, 1922 – March 1, 2019